WAR
BENEATH THE
WAVES

WAR
BENEATH THE
WAVES

A True Story of Courage and Leadership
Aboard a World War II Submarine

DON KEITH

NAL
CALIBER

NAL CALIBER
Published by New American Library, a division of
Penguin Group (USA) Inc., 375 Hudson Street,
New York, New York 10014, USA
Penguin Group (Canada), 90 Eglinton Avenue East, Suite 700, Toronto,
Ontario M4P 2Y3, Canada (a division of Pearson Penguin Canada Inc.)
Penguin Books Ltd., 80 Strand, London WC2R 0RL, England
Penguin Ireland, 25 St. Stephen's Green, Dublin 2,
Ireland (a division of Penguin Books Ltd.)
Penguin Group (Australia), 250 Camberwell Road, Camberwell, Victoria 3124,
Australia (a division of Pearson Australia Group Pty. Ltd.)
Penguin Books India Pvt. Ltd., 11 Community Centre, Panchsheel Park,
New Delhi - 110 017, India
Penguin Group (NZ), 67 Apollo Drive, Rosedale, North Shore 0632,
New Zealand (a division of Pearson New Zealand Ltd.)
Penguin Books (South Africa) (Pty.) Ltd., 24 Sturdee Avenue,
Rosebank, Johannesburg 2196, South Africa

Penguin Books Ltd., Registered Offices:
80 Strand, London WC2R 0RL, England

First published by NAL Caliber, an imprint of New American Library,
a division of Penguin Group (USA) Inc.

First Printing, April 2010
10 9 8 7 6 5 4 3 2 1

LIBRARY OF CONGRESS CATALOGING-IN-PUBLICATION DATA:

Keith, Don, 1947–
    War beneath the waves: a true story of courage and leadership aboard a World War II submarine/Don
Keith.
    p. cm.
Includes bibliographical references and index.
ISBN 978-0-451-22928-1
1. Billfish (Submarine).   2. World War, 1939–1945—Naval operations—Submarine.   3. World War,
1939–1945—Naval operations, American.   4. Rush, Charles W.   5. Submariners—United States—
Biography.   6. Unites States. Navy—Officers—Biography.   7. Courage—Case studies.   8. Leadership—
Case studies.   9. World War, 1939–19455—Indonesia—Makasar Strait.   10. World War,
1939–1945—Naval operations, Japanese.   I. Title.
D783.5.B55K45   2010
940.54'259838—dc22   2009047874

Set in Electra LH
Designed by Ginger Legato

Printed in the United States of America

For all the submariners who pulled the hatch
cover over their heads,
flooded the ballast tanks, and
swam beneath the wave tops on our behalf.

CONTENTS

Contents

WAR
BENEATH THE
WAVES

PROLOGUE

"Courage is resistance to fear, mastery of fear, not absence of fear."

—Mark Twain

S ubmariners who have survived an enemy's depth charge attack say it is almost impossible to describe to anyone else what the experience is like. Still, they feel obligated to try.

One sub sailor who lived through several poundings says, "It's like being somewhere south of hell with Old Scratch himself throwing bombs at you."

Some say the worst part is the sounds—the noises made by the warships above and by the charges themselves, and that does not just mean the explosions.

Those sounds can be clearly heard sometimes, even through the thick steel hull of a submarine, especially when the vessel is rigged for silent running. Water propagates sounds very well. Too well sometimes.

There is almost always the clacking of the enemy destroyer's screws as he crisscrosses the trail above, the Grim Reaper wielding his scythe, zigzagging relentlessly, honing in to claim his victims.

Then there is the nerve-racking *ping . . . ping . . . ping* as his sonar constantly, insistently probes the seabed below, looking for an echo back from his quarry that will tell him exactly where to drop his death.

Next, almost inevitably, there is the telltale *kerchug!* of the depth-charge barrels as they hit the water in a circle around where the enemy captain believes the submarine to be. That is followed at once by the increased frequency of the clack and whine of his screws as he pulls away to avoid the blow of his own ordnance.

Then a sharp *click!*—so much like the pop of a nearby lightning strike—that indicates the charge's fuse has reached the depth where it was instructed to detonate the ash can's powerful explosives.

There are sounds inside the submarine, too. Sounds that the sailors never forget.

The ragged breathing of a shipmate in the dim, dark quiet inside the boat—lights low to save precious battery power—as everyone nervously counts the time between *click!* and the inevitable explosion. Just as with the duration between lightning flash and thunder, the more time that passes, the better.

Then there is a noise described by some submariners as half a heartbeat. Maybe even an interrupted heartbeat. An odd sound that comes an instant before the deafening, bone-jarring *whoomp!* of the charge's detonation.

Depending on how close and where the explosion is in relation to the submarine, the hunted vessel might buck, sway, and slide violently sideways or tilt its nose downward or upward. Light-bulbs pop. Meter faces shatter into spiderwebs. Pipes tear loose from their clamps. Personal items and tools slide along the deck or spring from shelves. Dust and cork shower down from overhead like flour from a sifter. Leaks spray seawater all over a compartment with a high-pitched hiss. Water starts to seep in from myriad unseen places.

Sometimes, if the blast is especially vicious, the hull of the submarine might pull apart at a seam for an instant, just long enough to allow cold ocean to spew its way inside before the intense pressure of that same water closes the rent again.

Or at least, the crew prays it closes. Prays out loud or silently. It is hard to tell, because the blast leaves their ears deafened, ringing. Their murmured prayers add to the sounds, the awful sounds.

The crew tries to remain quiet, no matter how badly they want to yell and plead to God, or to the Japanese above, for it to stop. No screams or shouts in response are proper. Only mumbled prayers. Whispered orders. A quiet undertone of jokes as they whistle past the graveyard.

Even the slip of a wrench on a bolt or the squeak of a tightening pipe valve as the crewmen try to stem the inflow of the flood might be picked up by the attentive enemy above. That would be more than enough to give them a hint of where they are, to allow them to drop the next batch of deadly charges closer, deeper.

Some submarine sailors say the thing they most remember of those attacks is the pungent gumbo of smells. And the longer they remain imprisoned beneath the waves, the more that mixture simmers, the more a man has to struggle to suck enough breathable air into his lungs to stay lucid. To even stay conscious.

Sweat, diesel fuel, bilge fumes, acid from the batteries, foul air, oil, spilled food, human excrement and urine from the heads that vent inside while they are submerged, getting pounded. Then the prickly odor of a different recipe of gas when leaking seawater reaches and reacts with the chemical in the batteries.

And fear. Fear has a stench. Ask a man who has smelled it.

He may not want to talk about it, though. He always smells it on himself first.

Within about eight hours after diving, the atmosphere inside a World War II submarine begins to become difficult to breathe.

Longer and it becomes toxic, even explosive. Precious air becomes just as much a hazard to the men as the depth charges beating and boiling the sea around them.

All men are wired together differently. Some hold up better under such an attack than others. It is impossible to tell ahead of time which ones can and which ones cannot.

Most do not learn until the very first time it happens. And fortunately, most come through fine, concentrate on their jobs, do what they have to do to get them through and to safety. Even though they may fear they will crack, or they simply do not know, they perform admirably, shining brightly in a dark, desperate situation.

Others do not. They realize at the worst possible time that they simply cannot take it. No matter the simulations, the drills, it is simply more than they can stand.

There is no quiz or Rorschach test to verify ahead of time which man cracks, which man quietly does his job, which man steps ups and leads. It takes the real thing to do that, and by then, it may well be too late.

Submarine duty has always been and remains a volunteer service. Some, when faced with such terror, decide to serve their country in other ways. Others do not survive to make the move off the boats.

The success of the submarine navy in World War II verifies that most submariners shrugged off claustrophobia, misery, heat, choking air, gashes and bruises, and constant, cloying fear. They knew this would almost certainly happen when they signed on.

In a crisis, like a depth charging, they simply do the jobs they trained to do. There is no choice. Each man on board has a place to be—a station while on watch—and a duty to perform anytime he is there. If a man is hurt or overcome or cracks, another is supposed to be able to step into his station and take over. If they do their jobs correctly, they have a considerably better chance to survive the attack, even if they are deaf from the explosions, weak from fear, fatigued from struggling for breath, and bleeding and bruised from the tossing about the attack has caused.

Most try not to show that they are afraid, even when they accidentally piss themselves, inadvertently pray aloud, or whisper for their mothers when there is an especially close blast. Personalities change. Tough guys become weak. Meek men stand up and do heroic things.

Exceptional men assume command and lead the others.

They are all afraid, every last one of them. They are human. In most cases, they try not to judge those who do not hold up well during the attacks. Men who face death understand how small a distance it is from hero to coward. They are more tolerant of one another than someone who has not experienced it would be.

Deep below the surface of the ocean, they depend on one another when the depth charges fall and drift closer and closer to their hull.

Enlisted men, as they go about their jobs, assume the officers in the wardroom, the control room, and the conning tower know what they are doing. They take it for granted that the officers will make the right moves at the right time, give the best orders they can, and do whatever it takes to slip to safety before the enemy gets lucky, sneaks an ash can beneath them, and disembowels them. Before a charge rips off the sail and unleashes a horrendous flood from above. And it goes without saying that they trust their other shipmates to do their jobs, do them right, and go above and beyond when called upon.

Officers—from the skipper to the newest wet-behind-the-ears lieutenant right out of sub school—pray that their crew knows what to do to try to keep the boat in one piece until they can find a way out from beneath the rain of charges. They have to trust their men to do what they were taught in sub school, to hold firm, to not crack. Especially the chiefs, the most experienced among the enlisted men. The ones who will keep the youngsters in line with a glance, a word, a fistful of shirt under the chin, or an arm around the shoulders.

All of them—officer and enlisted man alike—hope the destroyer captain up there runs out of charges or patience before the submarine runs out of luck.

EARLY IN WORLD WAR II, the Imperial Japanese Navy had little success with their depth charges when used against a slippery American submarine force. There were other miscalculations. They had greatly underestimated the tactical power of the submarines, even as early as the attack on Pearl Harbor, when bombers concentrated on the battleships and left the submarine docks unscathed.

The United States had its own set of troubles—torpedoes that did not run true or explode when they were supposed to—so targets were scurrying away undamaged after a surefire attack. Still, through the first year of the war, U.S. submarine losses to depth-charge attacks were minimal. That was because the Japanese were arming them to blow up while they were still too shallow to do major harm. Most of the damage was to the crew members' nerves, not to their submarines.

Depth charges generated the greatest destruction when the drums blew up beneath the submarines' bellies. Skippers learned early to go to a safer depth, to at least 250 feet below the surface, and drive away using their relatively quiet battery-powered motors. Meanwhile, drums of TNT blew up nothing more than seawater and fish at a depth much shallower than where the submarines used to be.

Then, in June of 1943, the old adage about loose lips sinking ships proved tragically true. Congressman Andrew Jackson May, a Kentucky Democrat and a member of the House Committee on Military Affairs, was briefed on how the war was going by Navy brass during a trip to Pearl Harbor. That briefing included some sensitive information related to the submarine war.

Later, at a press conference, Congressman May divulged that the Japanese depth-charge tactics were not working. He did not stop there. He went ahead to tell reporters precisely what the enemy ship captains were doing wrong. The Japanese needed only to read the next morning's newspapers to learn exactly how they could more effectively pummel American submarines.

The commander of the Pacific submarine fleet at the time, Vice Admiral Charles Lockwood, later estimated that Congressman May's breach directly led to the loss of ten submarines and the lives of eight hundred men. May suffered no repercussions from his speech other than some bad press. However, the government later convicted him of an unrelated charge, accepting bribes from munitions suppliers.

In the summer of 1943, with the Japanese quickly becoming more effective in at least one phase of its antisubmarine warfare, a newly commissioned submarine named *Billfish* made her way to the Pacific and to war. Born at the naval shipyard in Portsmouth, New Hampshire, she was one of the new *Balao*-class ships that were being launched at a rate of a little better than one per month. Some observers at the time described this class of submarine as the most advanced war machine in history. *Balao* boats had a thicker hull and thus the ability to go deeper than previous submarines, well below four hundred feet. *Billfish* could dive deeper, travel farther and faster, carry more powerful deck guns, and be more effective against enemy shipping than any other submersible vessel ever built. Her radar and radio systems and her torpedo data computer (TDC) represented the very latest technology.

She was the perfect hunter and killer.

Her commissioning skipper—the captain who oversaw her construction and eventually took her to war—was a handsome Naval Academy graduate, class of 1930, from Chicago, Illinois, named Frederic Colby Lucas Jr. His résumé appeared to confirm his readiness to helm a state-of-the-art submarine. He had already been an officer on a surface ship—USS *Saratoga* (CV-3), an aircraft carrier launched in 1920—then went to submarine school in Groton, Connecticut. He eventually commanded USS *R-2* (SS-79), an old World War I–era submarine, built in 1917 and commissioned in 1918.

However, in reality, Lieutenant Commander Lucas had little actual submarine command background, and certainly not in wartime. Most of his experience was at the staff level, a desk job. In peacetime, that involved much more theoretical work than practical training for warfare. Even his lone submarine command—on R-2, which was a training boat by then—was very limited. He had trained for the proper way to mount a torpedo attack on an enemy target. He had trained for the procedures necessary to rig for silent running, how to maneuver a submarine during a depth-charge attack.

But he had never actually experienced any of it.

As with many others who received command of ships, squadrons, and other groups of soldiers and sailors, politics played a major role in Lucas's being chosen to helm *Billfish*. Any naval officer who wanted to work toward the rank of admiral had to know with which senior officers it was most advantageous to align himself, and Lucas knew how to play the game.

He was the son of a Harvard-educated botanist and high school teacher whose fondest hope was that his three sons would also attend Harvard. Though the younger Frederic Lucas attended the U.S. Naval Academy at Annapolis instead, his connection with the Ivy League stood him in good stead with many in the upper reaches of the Navy. There were many there who were impressed with anyone with ties to such a lofty educational background. That led directly to important positions and glowing reports on his service record.

Frederic Lucas was clearly on his way.

The Japanese changed the course of many things—including history and Frederic Lucas's carefully crafted career track—with the sneak attack on Pearl Harbor, Hawaii, in December 1941. Though many in America felt that war was inevitable, considering what was going on in Europe and the clashing of swords as Japan expanded its aggression around the Pacific, the United States was nowhere near ready for hostilities on such a grand scale and across such vast distances. Nor were many in her military ready for the kind of war that would be necessary if an enemy like Japan was to be defeated.

The U.S. Navy had a relatively small fleet of submarines at the time of the Japanese attack on Pearl Harbor. Still, their impact was felt quickly and mightily. Historians agree that the failure of the Japanese to bomb the submarine piers at Pearl Harbor was a major blunder. They concentrated on the battleships, ignoring the boats that were in port that day, as well as the big diesel tanks that held the fuel supply for them.

With the attack, America immediately entered the war. President Franklin Roosevelt, with a single order, also changed the way naval wars were fought by the United States when he declared un-restricted warfare. For the first time in our nation's history, warships had orders to sink any vessel that flew an enemy flag—military or merchant.

Only one month after Pearl Harbor, USS *Pollack* (SS-179) sank a Japanese freighter just out of Tokyo Bay. That was only the first of many.

By the end of the war, American submarines had sunk over half of the entire Japanese merchant fleet, creating a huge logistic prob-lem for them. Over half of all Japanese vessels dispatched to the bottom of the ocean, whether civilian traffic or warships, resulted from submarine attacks.

Submarines deprived the Japanese war effort of fuel and raw materials even as the Army and Marines recaptured lost territory and bombers pounded the homeland. With sea routes so effec-tively patrolled by American submarines, the Japanese economy was for all purposes strangled.

Along with many others, the war pressed Frederic Lucas into ser-vice in a position and a situation he may not have anticipated when he began his Navy career. Because he knew submarines, he found himself in the midst of what was suddenly a very hot conflict.

We have anecdotal evidence to support the notion that he was a reluctant draftee when he was called upon to put the brand-new *Billfish* into commission. It appears that he felt he could better serve the war effort in Washington or Hawaii. His evaluations indi-cated he had always done a fine job there. A fine job at the staff level.

Still, as a good officer must sometimes do, he accepted the com-mission and began preparing his new ship and crew as best he could. Besides, if a man aspired to become an admiral, a wartime combat command looked good on a résumé, too. That is, if he and his crew survived so he could make use of it.

Frederic Lucas was not the only one to find himself in a position he never actively sought. Officers with any significant submarine experience were scarce. The Navy called upon many of them to abandon their desks and take ships and men into harm's way, ready or not. Others with relatives in high places or with other convenient connections managed to end up with important positions—some in battle, some not.

Some did fine. Others did not. It happened in every branch of the service, not just the submarine Navy.

Additionally, at the beginning of the war, the Navy greatly favored older, more conservative commanders for its ships. For its highest command positions, too.

Never mind that some of them did not even understand the role of the submarine in modern warfare. Any captains who appeared too aggressive, who wanted to try new methods, were reprimanded, demoted, sent packing by the by-the-book squadron commanders and others higher up the organizational chart. They wanted skippers who would come back from patrol safely, their boats intact. Not younger, experimenting "cowboys" who pressed the attack and placed their boats and crews in needless peril.

Frederic Lucas fit the bill perfectly. He was an experienced, capable submarine captain, fresh from behind a desk and experience on the bridge of a training vessel. During the war, the Navy attempted to assign crew members to submarines so there was a mix of qualified, experienced sub sailors and those men who had recently graduated from sub school. Officers, too, were usually a blend of experience and new blood. A brand-new skipper was, whenever possible, teamed with an experienced executive officer

(XO). At the same time, most executive officers—the second in command on the submarine—were prospective captains.

The men who served aboard those submarines had no say-so in what kind of a leader they had for a skipper. Aggressive, conservative, experienced or not, they drew what they drew. Sure, that was happening in all branches of the service. Men were destined to serve under whomever blind luck and the brass gave them.

USS *BILLFISH* (SS-286), WITH LIEUTENANT Commander Frederic Lucas at her helm, was formally commissioned in April 1943. After completing hurried sea trials and intensive training for her new crew—including her captain—in the chilly waters of the Atlantic Ocean off New England, she made her way down the eastern seaboard, through the Panama Canal, and then across the Pacific Ocean for a stop at a quickly recovering Pearl Harbor.

By all accounts, sea trials went well. *Billfish* was a sturdy, capable ship with only minor new-boat glitches. Her crew took to her immediately and quickly jelled as a team. Her captain and his complement of officers seemed more than merely competent. Lucas knew the boat inside and out and led exercises and training with confidence and skill, challenging the crew to be precise and follow procedures exactly as the manuals dictated.

Second in command to Lucas, the boat's executive officer, was a battle-tested submariner, Frank Gordon Selby. Selby had already made two successful war patrols on USS *Silversides* (SS-236). His skipper there was Creed Burlingame, a colorful and bold commander and one of the war's early submarine heroes. Burlingame and his crew set records for tonnage sent to the bottom on several patrols, running his boat in an aggressive style. At the beginning of each attack, he rubbed for luck the belly of a small Buddha statue he kept close at hand. His daring assaults were a contrast to the conservative methods still being used by other commanders.

Selby absorbed much from Burlingame. He was excited about putting it to work against the enemy.

Like other warriors leaving home to face a vicious triumvirate of opponents, Lucas and his crew hardly had time to contemplate their fate. Like their skipper, few of them beyond XO Selby had any combat experience to speak of. Nor did they have any idea of how they might perform under the most intense pressure a human being could ever be required to endure. Those were not thoughts on which to dwell, though. Battle was inevitable. They enthusiastically prepared for it.

Their job assignment was clear. They were to kill.

Submarines were supposed to attack and sink warships, cargo vessels, tankers, or anything else that floated and flew the enemy flag. They were quite aware that there was a crafty, inspired war effort aimed right back at them, a navy that had a similar assignment. The crew of *Billfish* knew they might not live to make a return trip through the Panama Canal.

They were quite aware that many of their fellow submariners were already gone, on what sub sailors term "eternal patrol." *Billfish* docked in Pearl Harbor, on her way to Brisbane, Australia, for her first war patrol, in the summer of 1943, a year and a half into the war. By that time, sixteen American submarines—and more than a thousand American submarine sailors—had been lost.

Soon the crew of *Billfish* and her commander would face the enemy for the first time. Their suspicions about the tenacity of the Japanese, thoughts that went mostly unspoken, were to be confirmed quickly. It would not take them long to be tested in the most intense and telling way.

In three short months, on only her second war patrol, many of those men would find themselves in the midst of one of the most intense depth-charge attacks experienced by any vessel in World War II. Amid the unforgettable sounds, the soup of smells, and the stark reality of impending death, in that fifteen hours spent somewhere south of hell, heroes would be made and pretenders would be revealed.

There, beneath the waters of the Makassar Strait near Borneo, helplessly sealed inside a steel tube hovering hundreds of feet below a relentless enemy, the best and worst traits of those men would be exposed by the incessant *click!*, half a heartbeat, and *whoomp!* of the depth charges.

In the fetid, smothering air, in that incessant swirl of awful danger, the bravery and leadership of a dedicated group of young men became the difference between death and survival, while others, charged with leadership, were not up to the task.

For a number of reasons that I will make clear, this inspiring story remained untold for over sixty years. Indeed, that six-decade delay is another incredible facet of the tardy account of *Billfish's* saga.

Now, finally, we can learn of another shining example of how hellish war so often makes true heroes of otherwise common people. It is one of the most inspiring stories of courage to emerge from World War II, one well worth the wait.

It is unfortunate that most of those who lived it are no longer alive. One key performer in this play did not live to see the final act, the formal recognition that finally came his way sixty years after it happened, an award for bravery that was finalized about a month after he passed away.

As you read, though, keep this in mind: Regardless of how we might view the actions of some men with the luxury of safe, secure retrospect, it is important that we not judge any of them harshly.

Regardless of the incidences in question, all of these men were still part of an amazing record. Whether it was aboard *Billfish* that thunderous night or not, to a man they made a contribution to an effort that resulted in eventual victory.

No, this story is not being told to point fingers at those who failed. Instead, let us use this platform to honor those who stood up, who did their duty, who performed so valiantly in the harshest, most daunting circumstances anyone could imagine. Circumstances most of us could never imagine.

These men did what they trained to do. In the process, they won the war.

The war beneath the waves.

CHAPTER ONE

ON-THE-JOB TRAINING

"Cowards die many times before their deaths;
The valiant never taste of death but once."

—William Shakespeare

Charlie Rush came to submarines—and eventually to USS *Billfish*—because he got tired of eating his meals while standing up and was weary from only three or four hours' sleep each night.

That and the fact that the shotgun marriage between a ship's commander and a young officer on his first assignment turned out to be a stormy one.

Rush never regretted his choices—choosing the Navy over the Army, the military over civilian college and career, going from the surface Navy to the Silent Service—even though he experienced the best and the not-so-best of skippers along the way, regardless of what environment in which the vessel was designed to steam.

Rush was a bright young man, his potential obvious from an early age. He was Southern-born in Greensboro, a small farming town in west Alabama. He went to elementary and high school in Dothan, in south Alabama's "Wiregrass" area, after his family moved there when he was seven years old. He finished high school at the Gulf Coast Military Academy in Gulfport, Mississippi, not far from the big water of the Gulf of Mexico.

The Academy, founded in 1912, primarily prepared students for an Army career and specifically for admission to the U.S. Military Academy at West Point. Like many military academies, it had its share of troubled youngsters who did not do well in public school and were placed there for discipline and structure. That was not the case with Charles W. Rush Jr. He was there to prepare for a life as an officer.

Though Rush had the Army and West Point as an early goal, he took a decidedly different turn when he graduated Gulf Coast. Maybe it was the smell of salt water, borne on the southerly breeze off the Mississippi Sound, that changed his direction. He went to Annapolis instead of West Point, to the U.S. Naval Academy, to become a midshipman and eventually a naval officer.

Rush enjoyed life at Annapolis and looked forward to his service as an officer in the United States Navy when he graduated as an engineer. However, his time there was cut short by the Japanese sneak attack—the first by any foreign enemy on American soil—in Hawaii in December 1941.

The events of that awful Sunday reverberated throughout the Academy. War was something they studied in the classroom. History class and tactics class. Suddenly, with the reports on the radio, in the newspapers, and even in the newsreels at the movie theater down next to the piers in Annapolis, it was no longer an abstract subject. It was very, very real.

Rush's class went on immediate hurry-up, cutting the usual four-year matriculation to three. Naval officers were desperately needed, especially in the Pacific, and the academy did all it could to provide a steady supply of them. They double-timed classes, canceled leaves, and required students to show up for lectures and labs on weekends.

So it was that Charlie Rush found himself a commissioned naval officer almost a year short of his scheduled graduation date from the academy. Even more jarring, before the ink was dry on his diploma, he was immediately on his way from the classroom in Maryland to the Pacific and to war.

Despite the whirlwind way it happened, Rush was pleased when he tore open the envelope and saw that his orders sent him to serve as torpedo officer on a destroyer.

A destroyer is a versatile warship and can have many different duties, but Charlie Rush's first assignment was aboard one whose primary job was to protect one of the war's earliest hero ships, the aircraft carrier USS *Enterprise* (CV-6).

Enterprise had been involved in a great deal of warfare before Charlie Rush arrived aboard the destroyer that constantly shadowed her. *Enterprise*, with her crew of almost three thousand men, was at sea on December 7, 1941, on her way back to her home port at Pearl Harbor. Her mission had been to deliver a squadron of Marine Corps aircraft to Wake Island, just in case the Japanese lost their senses and attacked that distant outpost.

As they neared home, some of *Enterprise*'s scout planes arrived over Oahu in the midst of the Japanese assault. Enemy aircraft buzzed around the island like a beehive, and smoke and flames were visible from far out to sea. The scout plane pilots were stunned, but they immediately saw—and heard on the radio—what was going on. They promptly engaged the Japanese in dogfights directly over the smoke and fire the attackers had set loose.

When *Enterprise* got wind of what was happening, she got all remaining airplanes on her deck airborne, sending them off in search of the main Japanese attack fleet. They never located them. The war was on, though.

The carrier was soon involved in several major battles in the South Pacific. Most notably, her aircraft were part of the massive Doolittle bombing raid on Tokyo in April 1942, only four months after the attack on Pearl Harbor. That mission, despite a tragic loss of life among the bomber crews, was a tremendous morale booster for America.

Ironically, the bombers hosted by *Enterprise* dealt quite a bit of unintended grief to American submarines, too. Only two weeks after Pearl Harbor, aircraft from the carrier mistook for an enemy boat and bombed USS *Pompano* (SS-181) not far out of Pearl Harbor. Though none of the bombs hit directly, one especially close charge damaged the submarine's fuel tanks, and she had to limp home, trailing an oil slick behind her. She was fortunate to make it.

Enterprise aircraft also bombed the submarines *Thresher* (SS-200), *Sargo* (SS-188), and *Gudgeon* (SS-211) on different occasions later in the war. Fortunately, their aim was just bad enough in each case and no serious damage resulted from any of the incidents. Aircraft were especially notorious for not having the latest friend-or-foe identification codes. It was not unusual at all for submarine crews to have to deal with the added threat of attacks from friendly fire.

At least one submarine, USS *Dorado* (SS-248), was almost certainly sunk by a friendly aircraft in October 1943. Newly commissioned— and not far behind *Billfish* in traversing those same waters—she was on her way south to the Panama Canal when a patrol plane dropped bombs and depth charges on a submarine on the surface. The airplane's crew always maintained it was a German U-boat, spotted as it passed between Puerto Rico and the Dominican Republic.

Dorado never showed up at the Canal Zone. According to postwar records, no U-boats were lost during that time span and in that area.

A destroyer is a fast, maneuverable, and very deadly vessel. Its primary mission typically is to protect larger warships, such as aircraft carriers and battleships, or to run interference for either military or merchant convoys. The main threat to the bigger ships came from aircraft and submarines, so destroyers in World War II were equipped with radar, acoustic-detection gear, antiaircraft guns, and antisubmarine weapons, such as depth charges and torpedoes. Weaponry had to be especially adaptable and deadly, since attackers could be approaching by air, on the surface, or beneath the sea.

Destroyers, depending on their vintage and class, were about 350 feet in length, could travel very fast—35 to 38 knots (65 to 70 miles per hour)—and typically in wartime carried a crew of between 250 and 275 men.

Destroyer crews have always proudly referred to their ships as "tin cans," and to themselves as "tin can sailors." That is an apt name.

While not exactly expendable, the ships were designed to take ordnance intended for the battleship or carrier they protected, yet steam on, to live to continue fighting. They could have holes shot in them and still float and protect the larger ships behind them. Of course, their speed, maneuverability, and complement of weapons made them a deadly threat to enemy warships.

The quick development of the so-called DEs (destroyer escorts) by the United States and her allies, just before and during the early part of the war, made the destroyer an even more versatile warship and was a major contributor to the victory over the Germans and Japanese. The U.S. Navy really gained an advantage over the German U-boats when it began to deploy antisubmarine task groups consisting of a small aircraft carrier and a couple of DEs or cruisers. Planes off the decks of the carriers patrolled grids and spotted the U-boats from the air. The destroyers hurried to the area and, in more and more cases, successfully attacked and sank them.

Of course, the enemy had their own "tin cans" and submarine-hunter aircraft, which were more often launched from land bases controlled by the Japanese. Though lacking the range and sophistication of the American destroyers, they used their equipment and tactics very effectively against U.S. submarines in the Pacific, just as the Allies were doing in the Atlantic.

Charlie Rush was proud to be assigned to such a valuable naval asset, and he looked forward to serving his country in this way. He was especially excited to be aboard a vessel that was defending *Enterprise*.

It did not take long, however, for him to sour on the assignment.

His big worry was the captain under whom he would be serving. Certainly, as a new graduate from the Academy on his first duty, Rush had little power and no experience. There was no way, though, that he could express his reservations to anyone else concerning what he soon observed about the skipper of his destroyer and how he ran his ship. One simply did not criticize his superior officers. There is a fine line between bellyaching and insurrection.

And, after all, mutiny in wartime is a capital offense.

Still, from the very beginning of his time on the destroyer, Rush mentally questioned his new captain's readiness and suitability for the job. He was convinced the man might get them all killed.

Men who serve on ships have no vote on whom their superiors will be, any more than soldiers can choose their commanders or platoon leaders or airmen can pick their pilots or squadron leaders. Charlie Rush's new skipper was a graduate of Harvard, class of 1919, with no wartime experience at all. He was a steam engineer who spent more time idly working theoretical math problems or designing vents and piping for nonexistent ships than he did practicing antisubmarine warfare or running aircraft drills to prepare his crew and existing ship for battle.

The skipper seemed blithely unconcerned about such things. Tactics and training were of no interest to him.

That was not the only problem. Rush quickly noticed that the man had no leadership skills at all. The rest of the crew was well aware of it when Rush got there. He heard the rumblings, suppressed as they were. Yet they could do nothing about it either.

Even more discouraging, each time the ship returned to port after a patrol, their incompetent skipper routinely received commendations and glowing support from his bosses. Judging from the patrol endorsements from his superiors, the steam engineer was easily one of the war's best destroyer captains. Whether it was ignorance or the captain's political savvy, no one who counted seemed aware of the captain's inadequacy.

Everyone on board the destroyer knew the truth. They knew it was they and their executive officer who made the guy look good to those back at headquarters. And there was no easy way to make aware anyone who counted or who could make a change.

That would not be the only time that Charlie Rush encountered an officer who was so unsuited for his command, a skipper placed in a position for which he was not prepared based on political connections, or, as was often the case, because nobody better was available for the job.

The next time, though, he found a way to do something about it.

There was one bright light on his initial duty station. The executive officer on the destroyer seemed to be a competent officer. He was equally frustrated with their unfortunate draw of captains. However, when Charlie subtly approached him with his concerns about his new CO, the XO only shrugged and brushed him off.

"I know. I know," the XO told Rush, once he was sure no one else could hear their exchange. "Somebody up the chain of command sees 'Harvard' on an officer's résumé, that guy gets the bridge even if he can't even spell 'skipper.' We have a good crew here, but the old man won't allow me any authority. We get in a scrape, I'll do what I have to do to protect *Enterprise* and try to save our bacon while I'm at it."

"Do what you have to do? How far would you go, XO?" Rush really wanted to know if the exec would actually tell the commanding officer to stand down — or take even more drastic action.

The officer only shrugged again, quickly glancing around them again to ensure that nobody might overhear.

"Far as I have to go to do what has to be done."

Charlie thought about that conversation often during his long hours on duty. Would he back the XO if it came to it? That could mean an end to his naval career before it had even started. It could spell jail time or worse. But it could also be a matter of life and death, too.

It was also true that the fitness of his CO to command a ship was not all that bothered Charlie Rush about serving on the destroyer. On his first and only patrol aboard the "tin can," they were at sea for one hundred days. One hundred days and nights riding the wake, steaming through the bow spray of the aircraft carrier they were assigned to protect. Skittering across the wave tops like the spindly "snake doctors" who danced on the still water on the cattle ponds back in south Alabama.

They were constantly on the lookout, listening, watching the radar, using binoculars to search the sky and sea, scanning for aircraft that might be sneaking up on them from inside a tropical squall or coming out of the sun. Trying to catch a glimpse of a submarine's slender sliver of a periscope, a hint of smoke on the horizon that might be an approaching enemy gunboat. It was frustrating, nerve-jangling duty.

Though not quite seasick, Rush still stayed queasy most of the time he was on duty, his eyes stinging and his head aching from constantly scanning the horizon as the ship rocked unceasingly beneath his feet.

As torpedo officer, and as ordered by his CO, he was, quite simply, always on duty. At sea for one hundred days, he never once sat down for a meal. He ate standing up, usually at his duty station. One hundred nights and he never got more than three or four hours of sleep at a time before somebody was rousting him from his bunk, sending him back on watch.

He suspected there was a better way to handle duty such as his, but he knew better than to approach his commanding officer with any suggestions. Others, including the XO, had tried. Their input was not welcomed.

Rush did not mind hard work or discomfort. He was a farm boy, accustomed to long, difficult labor. But he knew he might not be his best in a tight situation if he was tired and hungry, sick and half-blind. Neither would the others with whom he served.

Charlie Rush had never quit at anything in his life, but when his convoy got back to Pearl Harbor, he immediately approached the duty officer and requested a change of scenery. Impulsively, and with only a little information to go on, he asked for submarines.

There would be complications, he knew. First, there was doubt he could even find an officer's spot on one of the boats. Surprisingly to some, it was desirable duty. It could be quite a while before a slot came open.

There was a certain scorn for the submarine service, too, among other Navy personnel. They called submarines "eel boats," "plunging boats," "devil divers," "pig boats," and worse. Submariners chalked it up to jealousy, but the attitude led to many fights at shore-leave hangouts.

No matter. He had already made up his mind. There were a number of compelling factors for why submarines became the course he wanted to set for the balance of his Navy career.

First was the simple fact that an officer lives and works side by side with his crew. With a typical complement of sixty or seventy crew members aboard the submarines of that era, and with all of them operating in such close quarters, an officer quickly learned the names of every man aboard. The names, the hometowns, the names of girlfriends, wives, and kids.

If he took the time, the officer also learned each crew member's strengths and weaknesses, whom he could count on and who might not be able to handle his job when things got rough. That aspect of submarine service greatly appealed to Rush.

He figured there was a chance for quicker advancement on the diesel boats, too. He was ambitious, sought greater responsibility, and there was plenty of demand for good submarine skippers in the "Silent Service." If the Navy was looking for other destroyer commanders like the one he was running away from, then Rush wanted no part of the surface Navy!

The pay was better, too. Ever since President Theodore Roosevelt took a ride in an early submarine, crews on the boats received higher wages than others in the Navy did. They drew the equivalent of hazardous-duty or combat pay all the time, not just when they were at war.

Even the food was superior on submarines. Everyone in the Navy knew that submariners enjoyed better chow—at least at the beginning of their patrols, before stores began to run low and a fresh orange was a luxury.

Rush assumed that meals were served sitting down, too, the way his mother insisted it be done back home.

Eating great meals while sitting at a table! What a way to fight a war!

There was admittedly a bit of glamour involved, too. Adventure.

The submariners tended to be a different breed, and their skippers were akin to fighter pilots, the Navy's equivalent of "aces." Some had already acquired reputations as "cowboys." To be sure, some operated too riskily for their own good. Others led with swagger and flamboyance, but they got the job done while, in the process, bringing their boats and crews home safely, even triumphantly, flying miniature Japanese flags they called "brag rags" and other banners.

Some of the submarine "aces" even tended to carry colorful names befitting their reputations. Names that rang like those of the chiseled-jaw heroes in action-adventure novels—"Red" Ramage, "Moke" Millican, Creed Burlingame, Dick O'Kane, Walt Griffith, "Mush" Morton, Slade Cutter.

There is a tendency to think of submarines as a relatively recent innovation, but that is not the case. Alexander the Great commissioned the building of a submersible vessel as a possible weapon of war. He took a dive in one over three hundred years before Christ, but it was little more than a diving bell, not designed to be propelled beneath the waves.

The first record of a diving boat with a propulsion system and guidance capability was an English effort in 1580. One hundred and fifty years later, more than a dozen submarines had already been patented in Great Britain.

Fast-forward to the Revolutionary War. For the first time, a submersible vessel was used in warfare. It was the *Turtle*, a one-man diving boat propelled by a hand-operated crank that spun a screw propeller. She slipped beneath the HMS *Eagle* and attempted to attach a cache of gunpowder to the British ship's bottom. *Eagle* had a tough copper sheathing protecting her keel and the submarine's pilot was unable to attach the explosives. The ability to get beneath an enemy warship without being detected had been proven, though, and it was only a matter of time before such an operation would be perfected.

Robert Fulton, whose name is more closely associated with the steamboat, built a workable submarine in the late 1700s, a decade before he developed the steam-powered surface ship for which he is better known. Fulton's submersible looked more like what we expect a submarine to look like, but no one seemed interested, especially in peacetime, in pursuing further development.

As is usually the case, war leads to technological advancement. By the time of the American Civil War, a number of experimental submarines were being tested. Crude by comparison to later ships, they often sank and claimed the lives of the men who were aboard them. The *Hunley* was a Confederate boat cobbled together using an old steam boiler and manned with a crew of eight men. This boat, too, relied on manpower to propel her. She submerged and entered Charleston Harbor in South Carolina in February 1864. Her mission was to ram a spar with explosives strapped to it into the side of a U.S. Navy warship, the *Housatonic*. *Hunley* and her crew were able to do that, and then, using foot paddles that drove the screw, they retreated to what they hoped was a safe distance and detonated the powerful charge. *Housatonic* sank on the spot.

Though exactly what happened next is still unknown, the Confederate submersible went down before she could return to her port farther up the coast. Her crew was lost, creating another submarine milestone that evening—though a dubious one—when *Hunley*'s crew became the first submarine sailors to die in battle.

Clearly, if submarines were to be serious warships, they needed a better propulsion system than men paddling or hand cranking the screws. Steam turned out to be the answer, and remains a part of what makes submarines go to this day. Only the way of heating the water to make that steam has changed.

In the late 1800s, though, the major obstacles to overcome were how to safely heat water to make the steam, what to do with smoke and heat that boilers produced, and how to store enough fuel—coal being the primary one—to stoke the fire to make the steam.

Still, even though the need for such a ship was accepted, the problems and compromises led to a lack of enthusiasm for the submarine among the world's navies. Then along came the improved electric motor. The first electric-powered submarine debuted in Great Britain in 1886, sporting two fifty-horsepower motors. The electricity to run it came from a one-hundred-cell storage battery, one that could be repeatedly recharged using the coal-fired steam engine to run a generator.

That was a major development, but there were still problems. The battery charge had to happen with the boat on the surface. And even with the breakthrough of a reliable, rechargeable battery, it still required frequent boosting, limiting both range of operation and the length of time a submarine could remain below the surface, hiding from a counterattack.

J. P. Holland, an American inventor, is generally credited with working through these types of limitations. After convincing the U.S. Navy to buy a submarine from him, he delivered his boat in 1900. The *Plunger* used the familiar dual methods of propulsion—steam while on the surface and storage batteries anytime she was submerged—but Holland's technology was far better than anything anyone had seen before. He developed other submarine innovations that are still in use, in some form or another, today, such as buoyancy tanks that could be flooded or evacuated to dive or surface. Holland also introduced the diving planes. These "wings" helped determine the angle of attack as a submarine varied its depth. This made it easier and safer for the boats to alter how deep they were while submerged or dive and surface smoothly, quickly, and somewhat reliably.

By the beginning of World War I, other innovations made the submarine a formidable naval asset. Sir Howard Grubb invented a practical periscope, giving submarine crews eyes on the surface while their ship remained mostly hidden. That was a major step toward being a stealthier and more dangerous adversary for surface vessels. The torpedo underwent more development and became a significant nautical weapon.

There were breakthroughs in what made a submarine go, too. Gasoline and diesel engines, their development driven mostly by automobile manufacturers and the railroads, became more reliable. Still, though, the boats had to do most of their traveling on the surface and were forced to keep short-time batteries charged in case they needed to remain below the surface for any period of time.

But batteries were also undergoing changes. They now held a bigger charge and lasted longer, so submarines could hide and attack more efficiently than ever before.

By 1912, all U.S. Navy submarines used diesel engines and batteries. Diesel engines, primarily developed for locomotives, required no complicated sparking systems and produced less dangerous fumes than gasoline-powered power plants. Less dangerous fumes, but they still put off enough bad stuff that they remained a threat to submariners all the way to the nuclear era.

The United States Navy had two dozen submarines in its fleet at the start of World War I. The admirals that ran the Navy were of the opinion that they were suitable only for patrolling harbors and coastlines and, possibly, escorting surface ships when they made short runs. The consensus was that the "plunging boat" was, at its best, a defensive weapon with limited use in warfare. There was a decided surface-ship bias in the Navy of the time. The Germans and their aggressive U-boat skippers changed many of their minds.

Still, some felt the Navy should be concentrating instead on battleships and the new favorite of many of the top admirals, the aircraft carrier. Submarines, on the other hand, were still considered to be too slow and too dangerous. Even so, development and modernization of submersible vessels continued, even as peace settled over the world.

Once again, it would take war to propel the technology forward.

THOUGH HE WAS ANXIOUS TO make the move to submarines, Rush figured that even if his request was honored, he would have at least one more long patrol on the "tin can." One more voyage spent bobbing alongside *Enterprise* with "Captain Steam Pipe" before he would be able to make the change.

And then he would have a stint back at the Navy's submarine school on the banks of the Thames River in Groton, Connecticut. Even after he graduated from sub school, he would soon have to qualify in submarines. Men who have submarine duty are required to have knowledge of all duty stations on the boat and be able to step right in should another man become incapacitated. The qualification process—especially for an officer—was arduous, but resulted in a well-cross-trained crew. Success in qualifying was signified by being allowed to pin on the twin-dolphins insignia— silver for enlisted men, gold for officers.

Sub sailors were (and still are) usually required to graduate from submarine school, and often had to attend other special schools to learn more about the engines, radio operating procedures, the submarine electrical system, sonar, or whatever their specialty was going to be. They combined classroom learning with actual onboard training. When they were assigned to their first boat, they had to be trained some more, until they could qualify. The alternative for those who were not able to qualify within a reasonable time was assignment to other duty, either ashore or on a surface vessel. Incidentally, a similar qualifying procedure is still in place today, even though the jobs on the boats have undergone quite a transformation.

It is important to note that service aboard submarines in the U.S. Navy is and always has been voluntary. No one has ever been drafted into the Silent Service. The Navy recognizes that it takes a special breed of man for such duty, and not all those who volunteer make it. There are duty stations in which the failure of one man to properly perform his job could easily result in the loss of the ship and its crew. And by its very nature, not everyone is prepared for the unique nature of submarine duty. Anytime any submarine sailor wishes to "unvolunteer," his request is honored, no questions asked, and it does not negatively affect his service record.

Rush figured he would worry about going to sub school and earning his dolphins when the time came. First he had to get the transfer, then suffer through another run on the tin can.

To his surprise, though, he immediately drew an assignment to a submarine. For once, the desperate shortage of officers—especially engineering officers—worked in his favor. Even more surprising, he would not head back to the States for sub school after all. There was one particular submarine that needed an engineering officer and it needed one right now, before she left on the next run.

Charlie Rush had never even been aboard a submarine for

more than a few minutes. Now he was about to steam away on a war patrol aboard one of those odd, black, slippery vessels. He was thrilled, even if he was about to draw duty on one of the ships that the surface Navy snidely referred to as "sewer pipes" or "pig boats."

He was, unbeknownst to him, about to get away from a less than adequate commanding officer and have the opportunity to serve with one of the very best in the U.S. Navy. He would have been even more excited about his new job if he had known who his boss would be and how great a teacher he was.

Rush was headed to the USS *Thresher* (SS-200). His new skipper was none other than William John "Moke" Millican, one of those "cowboys" about whom everybody was talking. Unlike some of the others, though, Millican was one of the "aces" who had earned the respect and admiration of even the toughest old-line squadron commanders. Yes, he was aggressive and preferred his own way of running a submarine patrol, but he brought his ship home, its crew alive.

When Rush reported for duty aboard *Thresher*, he felt an obligation to make sure his new CO knew the truth, that there had been no mistake. He confessed to him that he had not yet attended sub school. He also let Millican know that he had little experience with these complicated, diesel-electric-driven undersea predators.

"Don't worry, Charlie," Millican told him with a broad, welcoming smile and a slap on the back. "Come with us and you'll get a better education on *Thresher* than they could ever give you back there in sub school."

Millican was not exaggerating. Charlie Rush was about to get the best on-the-job training any submariner could ever obtain. Even so, Rush broke out the manuals and began studying the systems for which he would be responsible. He learned from the men who were experts already, usually the chiefs, the longest-tenured enlisted men. That was the most obvious way to get crash-course training in how the fleet boats worked—called "fleet boats" because of the long-held belief that the submarine's primary purpose was defensive, protecting fleets of "true offensive warships" like the aircraft carriers and the battleships.

It was training that would, in only about a year, serve Charlie Rush well. What he learned at Millican's elbow would enable the young officer to help save the lives of himself and the rest of the crew of another submarine. A submarine that would be in about as bad a spot as he could have ever imagined.

Such thoughts were far from his mind, though, when Rush walked across the brow and onto the deck of USS *Thresher* for the first time, ready to proudly ride her off to war as a bona fide submarine sailor.

CHAPTER TWO

HOOKED!

"I dragged my gear down to the shore and saw the submariners, the way they stood aloof and silent, watching their pigboat with loving eyes. They are alone in the Navy. I admired the PT boys. And I often wondered how the aviators had the courage to go out day after day, and I forgave their boasting. But the submariners! In the entire fleet they stand apart."

—James A. Michener, *Tales of the South Pacific*

W illiam "Moke" Millican was the antithesis of the hesitant, conservative submarine skippers who commanded
many of the boats early in World War II. A member of
the Annapolis class of '28, he was short but stocky and athletic, an
Irishman from a small town on Long Island, New York. He was a
championship boxer at the Academy who considered a relentless,
bold attack as his strong suit when he faced an opponent in the
ring.

Hesitation, he felt, only invited a strong counterpunch.

Like Charlie Rush, his new, green engineering officer, Millican
was dismayed by the way many naval captains ran their boats. Dismayed but not surprised. The truth was, since the earliest days of
submarines, the Navy taught captains a simple strategy. They were
to avoid contact with the enemy until they were in the perfect position to launch an attack. They were supposed to use their stealth to
hide, to avoid conflict that would give away their presence too early
in the assault, and to strike only when success was a certainty.

Some submarine commanders took that dictum to extremes.
They literally ran away from good targets. Whether that was simply

43

following clearly defined procedure or something that bordered on cowardice is best left to conjecture.

There was also the matter of "unrestricted warfare." By treaty, the United States was forbidden from attacking merchant ships in international waters. Captains and crews of all vessels—including submarines—were trained to target only warships. Tactics learned and practiced were to be used only against military vessels.

Suddenly, within hours of the Pearl Harbor attack, those treaties and the corresponding tactics were jettisoned like bags of garbage over the side. Ships and submarines were to engage in "unrestricted warfare" at the order of the commander in chief, President Franklin Roosevelt. The United States would be a good two years into the war before many of its naval commanders were comfortable with this new type of warfare, not only the concept but the tactics needed to be successful at it.

It was especially crucial that submarine commanders understood what "unrestricted" meant and how to conduct such fighting. Of all the Navy's ships, their vessels were best suited for the exact kind of war that was now being fought—a war in which a tanker filled with oil or a freighter whose holds were crammed full of bauxite or rubber was an even more crucial target than a gunboat or a cruiser. Many of them never comprehended this sea change.

"Moke" Millican, on the other hand, understood all this very well. Since becoming a submarine officer, he had served on a couple of the old "S" boats, enduring the worst equipment and environment imaginable. These were primitive, World War I–vintage submarines. He commanded *S-18* (SS-123), launched in May of 1920 and based at Dutch Harbor in the Aleutian Islands of Alaska. Conditions were horrible. The weather often prevented the crew from taking navigational fixes. Ice froze periscopes to the point they were unusable. Simply walking on icy decks was a hazard and many crew members were injured. Habitability aboard the boats was terrible, too, with poor heat, equipment malfunctions, and days without seeing the sun.

It was a frustrating way to try to fight a war.

So when Millican assumed command of USS *Thresher* in Pearl Harbor, Hawaii, in June of 1942, he took a different tack from many of his fellow skippers, regardless of the directives from higher up. He was tired of fighting his own equipment and the miserable elements. He was ready to vent some of that pent-up frustration on the enemy instead.

He was very impressed with his new vessel. It was much bigger than his previous boat, inside and out. The fact is, when afloat on the surface, most of a submarine lies below the water. They are very similar to an iceberg, with only the decks, the top of the conning tower, and the bridge and shears visible.

The shears, which gave the World War II–era submarine its distinctive appearance, are the radio and radar antennas, periscope housings, searchlight, flagpoles, and lookout stands that tower high above the decks and water. They are directly above the bridge. Height above the water was important for two reasons. First, it gave the lookouts a better view of the horizon. Second, it got the radio and radar antennas as high in the air as possible so they could launch a better signal and pull in weaker ones.

While the interior of *Thresher* was much more spacious than Millican's old boat, it was still cramped and confining compared to surface ships. Where did all that room go? It is because diesel tanks, ballast, and many other tanks, most designed to withstand tremendous water pressure, make up a huge portion of the vessel. These boats covered a vast range with few opportunities to refuel, so they had to carry a large amount of diesel fuel. Running out of gas was not an option. A submarine out of diesel and dead in the water was an easy target for enemy ships or aircraft.

The ballast tanks were also a necessity for depth control. Flooding the tanks with seawater would force the submarine to dive or go deeper. Venting—using compressed air to flush out the water—decreased depth or surfaced the ship completely.

Thresher and her sisters were about the length of a football field, including one end zone—311 feet from bow to stern. They were about twenty-seven feet wide at the broadest point. These submarines could safely dive to about four hundred feet, a specification termed the "test depth." They were able to steam at twenty knots while they were on the surface but only about nine knots maximum when submerged. Depending on speed, time spent on the surface and submerged, and a long list of other factors, these submarines had an approximate range of eleven thousand nautical miles and typically stayed on patrol for up to about seventy-five days, burning over a hundred thousand gallons of diesel fuel.

These boats carried eight to ten officers and between sixty and seventy enlisted men. It was tough duty. Few of them got to climb the ladders to spend time on the narrow, slippery decks, getting sun and fresh air. The bridge was cramped and usually occupied by the captain and diving officer. Two or three younger sailors—because of their assumed better eyesight—were on the tiny perches in the shears, keeping lookout. When the deck guns were used, those crew members assigned to the gun crew came topside. But most crew members went for long periods of time without sunshine or clean air. And they did it without touching land while on patrol in enemy-controlled waters, in seas that were often storm-tossed, and while they were constantly under threat of attack from surface ships, aircraft, floating mines, and other submarines.

It was dangerous to have too many men on deck while on the surface in enemy waters. Should the submarine have to dive in a hurry, there was typically less than a minute for everyone to get belowdecks. Almost always, the only hatch open was the one from the bridge downward to the conning tower. As the ship submerged, that hatch had to be cleared and its watertight cover closed before seawater reached it. Otherwise there was the risk of flooding the ship and sinking. That meant leaving men topside if everyone did not get below quickly enough.

There was little chance of recovering anyone if that happened.

During World War II, submarines had a variety of jobs to do. They were asked to observe, look for enemy shipping, sink those ships, perform lifeguard duty, deliver men and equipment into hostile places, transport and deploy mines, and more. But primarily, they were designed and built to attack and destroy enemy ships. *Thresher* and her sisters were especially well equipped for that purpose.

In addition to torpedoes, the submarines carried various weapons on their decks as well, including machine guns and small cannon. The captain usually had the opportunity to choose during construction what type of deck guns he wanted on his boat. Despite the assumption by many that subs did their damage only with torpedoes, many enemy vessels were damaged and destroyed using the boats' deck guns as well. As it turned out, these weapons were used quite often in furious, close-range combat, especially by aggressive warriors like "Moke" Millican.

There is often confusion about why these submarines are interchangeably called "diesel boats" and "electric boats."

While on the surface, four big diesel engines—very similar to those that drove diesel locomotives of that era—indirectly powered the vessel. Rather than actually turning the screws at the stern of the boat, the engines provided power directly to a generator and two electric motors that were, in turn, attached to twin screws that did the heavy work of propelling them through the water. Those big diesel engines also charged huge banks of storage batteries located in two separate compartments in the submarine's belly.

Those batteries were a key part of the propulsion system. They gave the boat electricity for the motors so she could run relatively quietly and without smoke when she was submerged. They also provided power for all the boat's systems: lights, radios, radar, and the like.

When the submarine was below the surface, the diesel engines were off. Motors, lights, sonar, instruments—everything electrical—got power from those batteries.

That is why this type of submarine is often referred to as an "electric boat" in one breath and a "diesel boat" in the next.

When the boats were at sea, diving was done daily in order to adjust the trim of the boat—its attitude in the water—as well as to determine the salinity of the water at different depths. A wartime dive could be completed in thirty to forty-five seconds if necessary.

When a submarine starts to dive, it causes a shifting of the center of gravity and the center of buoyancy of the vessel. There is a point where the center of gravity of the boat coincides with the center of buoyancy, and the goal was to get past that point quickly. If a wave were to hit the boat from the side at that moment, the submarine could actually be flipped over.

The diesels had to be stopped when the boat went into a dive. The intakes for air and the openings that released exhaust gases and smoke were closed. The speed was usually reduced to about three knots to save the precious battery power. Though these vessels could go as much as nine or ten knots while beneath the surface, they did it only for very short periods of time or in the case of an emergency.

The amount of battery power available was one determinant of how long they could remain submerged. How much air was left for the crew to breathe was the other limiting factor. When off watch while submerged, crew members were encouraged to relax in order to cut their consumption of air. In battle, though, all hands were required to be alert and ready to go to work.

When it came time to surface the submarine, the Klaxon would sound three short blasts to alert everyone on the boat about what was happening. High-pressure air was routed to the ballast tanks to blow water from them and outside into the surrounding sea. The air took its place, making the boat more buoyant. The planesmen would manipulate the bow and stern planes so that the boat would begin to make a controlled rise to the surface.

Once it was above the water, the conning tower hatch was opened so that any excess air pressure that may have built up in the boat could escape, equalizing the pressure inside the boat with that on the surface outside.

While this was going on, the main induction valves—the vents that allowed air to be routed to the engines—were opened and the diesels were cranked off.

While the systems on *Thresher* were designed to do similar tasks to those on his former submarine, Millican was more than happy with the advances that had been made from the old boat to the new one. He was pleased with his crew, too.

Only a lieutenant commander at the time and still in his mid-thirties, he was the "old man" on his ship in more ways than one. His crew was mostly in their teens and early twenties. It was not uncommon for young men of sixteen to lie about their age and have their parents go along with the ruse, confirming that they were seventeen and eligible to enlist. The average age of a U.S. Navy submarine crew member early in World War II was twenty-two.

Millican wanted to make certain his young crew was aware of what he intended to do with his new boat. Once *Thresher* was out of sight of the green Hawaiian coast and under way on her first patrol under his command—her fourth since she arrived in the Pacific—Millican picked up the microphone for the 1-MC all-boat public-address system. He was about to give his crew some good news and make them a solemn promise.

"Men, we have been assigned to a new squadron and we will be taking *Thresher* to Fremantle in Western Australia," he told them. "Our squadron commander is Rear Admiral Lockwood."

One crew member, Torpedoman Billy Grieves, later reported that the crew was elated with the change of scenery their skipper promised them. U.S. aircraft had twice mistakenly attacked *Thresher* since she had been in commission and operating out of Hawaii, including the bombing by aircraft flying off the decks of *Enterprise*. She narrowly escaped getting herself sunk by friendly fire each time. Other submarines had similar close calls in waters around and west of Hawaii, either from aircraft or surface units. There would be no such problems at Fremantle-Perth, located on the remote southwest coast of Australia.

The crew figured it was better to be in waters where the greatest danger came from the Japanese than to risk getting themselves laced by friendly fire. Besides, every man had heard about the friendliness of the Australian people, and especially their beautiful young women.

"We were not sorry to leave this area of the Pacific," Grieves wrote.

Grieves also noted that the crew immediately liked the attitude of their new skipper, especially his words on the 1-MC that day.

"Men, with your help, we will be aggressive in engaging the enemy at every turn," Millican promised them. "But I also promise you that I will not be foolhardy in that pursuit. We will do as much damage to enemy shipping—naval and commercial—as we can without taking needless and unnecessary risks. We will take the battle to the Japanese but we will take *Thresher* back to Fremantle in one piece."

That was precisely why most of those men enlisted and chose submarines. Now they had a skipper who promised them a chance to do it.

Thresher had already seen three war patrols under her first captain. On the third run, she, like the aircraft carrier *Enterprise*, was supporting the Doolittle raid on Tokyo. Before Doolittle's aircraft were ever launched, *Thresher* came under a hellish twelve-hour depth-charge attack. It was easily the most vicious of the war to that point. Still she stayed on station to relay intelligence and perform lifeguard duty for any of Doolittle's downed air crewmen who might require rescue.

The events, though, were more than her skipper at the time could stand. He decided he could serve his country and the war effort better in some other capacity. When *Thresher* finally limped back to Hawaii, her captain was one of the first men off the boat. He marched directly into the office of his squadron commander and told him he did not want to skipper a submarine anymore. From there, he went back to the States to run the submarine repair facility at Mare Island near San Francisco.

It took him three patrols and a brutal depth-charge attack, but the man finally realized he was not cut out to be a submariner, that he was risking his own life and that of his crew if he continued. To his credit, he decided to serve his country in another way before the worst happened.

That unselfish decision by the submarine's skipper was what brought "Moke" Millican to the bridge of *Thresher*.

Although he did not mention it to the crew, Millican did tell his officers how pleased he was that he was to be working for Charles Lockwood, too. They shared a similar vision for how a submarine skipper was supposed to run his boat. He looked forward to serving in his squadron, even if it was located in a remote part of the world, a long journey away from where most of the action was. Millican, after a tour in the Aleutians, was more than familiar with being out of the mainstream, but the weather in Western Australia was much, much better. And so was his submarine when compared to S-18.

So much for safer waters. Before they even got to Australia, they fell under two ferocious depth-charge attacks after stopping their transit to sink some enemy ships. During one incident, Millican had to take *Thresher* down in a hurry when the Japanese pressed the attack. Before the lookouts left the bridge, they were close enough to the enemy vessels so that they could hear men on the decks of the enemy ships shouting to one another.

But when *Thresher*'s decks were awash and they were only seconds from full submersion, a sudden flood of seawater poured down the hatch, drenching everyone in the conning tower. One of the men coming down from the bridge had lost his shoe in the rush to get belowdecks. It was enough to jam the hatch cover and keep it from closing tightly. They had to stop the dive, partially surface, clear the cover, and then head deep again.

That delay allowed the enemy destroyers to arrive on the scene, locate them, straddle them, and pummel them for several hours.

Then *Thresher* and her crew suffered one of the most harrowing experiences a submariner could ever endure. Some claimed to have nightmares about it for the rest of their lives.

It happened while they were still on their way to their new squadron headquarters in Australia, and even before their first full patrol under "Moke" Millican was complete. He had radar and sonar scanning for targets between Kwajalein and Wotje atolls near the Marshall Islands, determined to arrive at their new base with no torpedoes left.

Sonar and radar technology was rapidly evolving out of necessity, and while this technology was primarily developed for surface ships, its application in submarines was inevitable. Sonar employs transmitted and reflected underwater sound waves to detect and locate submerged objects or to measure distances. Its distinctive *ping! ping! ping!* is familiar to anyone who has watched a submarine movie. The sonarman spends much of his time on duty listening, not only to the emitted pings of his own sonar equipment, but also to the other noises that are conducted by seawater, sometimes from great distances. With his headphones strapped to his head, a good sonar operator can determine considerable detail about a ship contact that may be a long way from his position. Minor sound differences, such as a worn ball bearing in a propeller shaft or bubbles at the bow of a ship, allow a sonarman to identify and track multiple vessels at once. He also listens for the sounds that indicate an aggressor has launched an attack. He hears torpedo tube doors opening or torpedoes in the water, hopefully quickly enough to allow for evasive measures. Radar, on the other hand, uses radio signals to detect objects at a distance. That technology continued to evolve throughout World War II. More sophisticated radar on all fronts—including aboard submarines—and the delay of the Japanese in obtaining more advanced technology turned out to be a key factor in the Allied victory. For submarines, radar could be used only when the antenna was poked above the surface of the water. It had no use while the ship was submerged. Millican and his crew paused in a narrow pass between islands long enough to sink a torpedo tender ship, *Shinso Maru*.

Once again, thunderous explosions rocked them as they dived

to hide in the shallow water. This time, though, it was not depth charges from a destroyer. It was a well-placed bomb as well as some dangerously close depth charges, and this time they came from an airplane that caught them as they submerged. Then, based on the sudden sounds of a destroyer's screws ratcheting away above them, they could tell that the enemy once again had them dead to rights.

No doubt the airplane summoned help to finish off the American submarine. In the close quarters of the pass, odds were very much with the enemy destroyer.

Suddenly, though, the sea above and around them grew eerily quiet. The rumbling explosions stopped. So did the frenzied spinning of the destroyer's propellers, now reduced to an almost gentle *clack, clack, clack*, as if he were simply marking time over them.

Had he given up the brawl that easily? Or was he only drawing back his fist to throw a knockout punch?

Millican and his crew in the control room looked at one another, wondering what the enemy was up to. They had *Thresher* effectively trapped in the passageway between the islands. They could go no deeper or risk getting stuck in the mud on the bottom. The aircraft soaring overhead could probably see them in the clear water and continue bombing them or tell the destroyer precisely where to drop its charges.

The quiet began to grate on their nerves as certainly as the thunder of the depth charges would have.

Millican was busily looking for a way out before the enemy captain decided to blast them. But no matter which way the *Thresher* turned, propelled by her quiet, battery-powered electric motors, the destroyer turned with them. The enemy ship stayed right above, shadowing them, as if attached by an unseen umbilical.

Still, the waters of the pass remained hushed—no more grumbling, teeth-rattling depth charges—like the calm before a particularly deadly storm. Only the gentle, watery shuffle of the destroyer's engines directly overhead. The crew went about fixing the things that broke with the first attack from the aircraft, still anticipating the telltale splashes of depth charges in the water in a circle around them.

What *Thresher* and her new skipper did not know at the time was that the initial close-by explosion damaged one of their compressed air tanks, one used to store high-pressure air needed to flush torpedoes from their tubes. It leaked a trail of tiny air bubbles to the surface, a perfect marker for their position. The aircraft could no longer see them in the murky water.

Even so, the destroyer crew knew exactly where its target was. She could remain right above them, following the bubbles through any evasive maneuvers the submarine might make while trying to slip away.

So why were they not pounding the American vessel? *Thresher* and her puzzled crew were about to find out.

Rigged for silent running, the inside of the submarine was as near completely quiet as seventy men could make it. They could hear the screws of the destroyer making a wavering drone above, the noise of the enemy ship even more pronounced without the splashes, clicks, and explosions of depth charges. Their faces shiny with sweat, those who were not doing something that required their eyes to focus downward looked up instead, as if they could determine the enemy's intent if they stared at the hull over their heads hard enough.

Then, suddenly, a loud, metallic *clank* shattered the silence! Something hard and heavy on the starboard side, somewhere near the bow.

At first, the men thought they might have struck something, maybe even another submarine, but there had been no sonar indication of an obstruction in their path. The boat still swam smoothly forward, looking for a way out.

No sign of a collision. No rip in the hull. No flood of water. But what was that noise?

Again the men in the control room all looked at one another, then upward, but no one ventured a guess.

Then the piercing, clanking noise rang out again, like a clapper striking the inside of a giant bell. The harsh, metallic noise reverberated the length of the submarine. Next, it melded into a ragged, piercing, scraping sound, running slowly down the length of the submarine from the bow toward the stern, like the shrieking of an angry banshee. It passed each man working on the starboard side of the submarine, making its way all the way down the outside of the hull.

Then the hellish racket stopped as suddenly as it had started when it reached a point on the hull just outside the aft torpedo room, near the very back of the vessel.

Jesus! What *was* that?

Each man looked at his shipmates, wondering if maybe they had cruised past and brushed against a sunken hulk without somehow bouncing a sonar ping off it. Or maybe they had encountered a submerged mine that had—so far—miraculously failed to explode. Or had they actually snagged the chain of a mine, and were about to tow it along with them until it did blow them to kingdom come?

The grating noise was frightening enough, but everything else seemed normal. Except for the continued absence of attack by the destroyer that still clattered away three hundred feet over their heads.

"Captain, something's wrong with the stern planes," the sailor who was operating those controls reported in a remarkably calm voice. "They must have been damaged when . . ."

The planes on a submarine act similarly to flaps on an airplane, controlling the angle of attack the boat takes through the water. Like wings, they enable the planesman to bring the stern of the ship down or up as necessary to keep the sub from diving or surfacing too abruptly and thus losing control. They also enable him to keep the boat at a steady, level angle—"maintain the trim"—when they cruise along while submerged. Losing control of a plane in these shallow waters, with angry bees buzzing around on the surface, was a very serious development.

Suddenly they lost the influence of the planes completely. The controls would not budge. The diving officer noticed something else worrisome.

The stern of the boat was definitely starting to rise as the bow began to point decidedly downward. The decks beneath the crew's feet tilted more and more toward the bow and the sea bottom.

Something powerful had hold of them. It was trying to pull them to the surface by the tail!

It was clear then that a grapnel of some kind had them hooked like a very big fish. Their lip was the stern plane on the starboard side.

Millican quickly deduced that the giant fishhook had snagged the now inoperative stern plane on that side of the boat after scraping all the way down their side. That was why it no longer worked.

While on the surface, a submarine in *Thresher's* class displaced fifteen hundred tons, which made her quite heavy. However, while submerged, she was relatively light. Even a small ship, with a strong winch, chain, and grappling hook, would have a good chance of successfully dragging her to the surface.

Millican and his crew quickly realized that this was exactly what was happening to them!

The enemy did not intend to blow them to kingdom come after all. He was intent on capturing an American submarine and her crew and everything she carried, especially the top secret documents and codebooks locked in the safe in the captain's stateroom and in the radio room.

Every man looked to their new skipper. Millican's actions in the next couple of minutes could mean escape or capture, freedom or torture or death. In the back of every man's mind was the thought, Would the "old man" allow the ship to be captured, or would he order the detonation of the torpedoes and scuttling charges and kill them all before he allowed that to happen?

Would he sacrifice the boat and crew to prevent the enemy from capturing *Thresher*, its crew, its confidential paperwork and top-secret codebooks? Or would he allow them all to be captured?

"All ahead emergency!" Millican barked. "Planesmen, hard dive! Hard dive!"

While there was urgency in his commands, there was no panic. He was going to do what he could to get away first; then he would make that life-or-death decision that loomed ahead if he failed.

Millican had just ordered the motors rammed into overdrive and for the men on the planes to steer their ship on a dive toward the bottom of the sea, which was not that far ahead of the bow. The entire submarine shuddered and groaned with the strain as the twin screws grabbed water and tried to pull them free from the grapnel's firm grip.

The depth gauges showed that despite the tremendous energy expended by the motors, the enemy ship on the surface still dragged them upward toward capture.

The batteries could not supply enough voltage to keep the

screws churning long at that rate. And if they ran out of juice, there was no way to prevent them from getting reeled in.

Millican ordered, "All stop."

He then told the crew to flood all tanks with seawater, and even to flood the torpedo room bilges until water was up to the deck plates, where the men stood watch, ready to fire their weapons if called upon to do so. Maybe, by making *Thresher* as heavy as they could, they had a chance to snap the chain or break the hook and get themselves loose.

No such luck. The depth gauges showed they had been dragged upward past two hundred feet already and they were still going up. But now it was at a decidedly steeper angle. It was only a matter of minutes before their rear end and the impotently spinning screws were near the surface of the channel and they were being dragged to shore.

Even as the captain tried again to wrench their way free with the boat's powerful motors—to no avail—he ordered the crew to set the scuttling charges and destroy as much secret information as they could. Several men lashed drums carrying fifty-five pounds of TNT between the torpedoes in each torpedo room, ready to blow at the right moment, to destroy *Thresher*. Maybe, if they made a big enough bang at just the right time, they could take with them the sons of bitches who were reeling her in.

One hundred and fifty feet, the depth gauges read, and the diving officer called out the numbers to confirm the bad news.

The ascent angle was even sharper, the boat's nose pointed sharply downward. Objects not secured rolled down decks and crashed noisily into bulkheads. No one worried about the enemy hearing the noise now. Men braced themselves against anything solid to keep from being thrown forward.

There was only one other thing to try. Spit out the hook!

"Flood forward!" Millican ordered.

That filled the last available space with heavy seawater. And that dramatically increased the boat's weight, making the downward angle even more pronounced, virtually standing them on their nose. Everyone grabbed whatever he could find to keep from being thrown forward against something hard or sharp.

"Left full rudder! All ahead emergency!"

Each man did his job and his captain's bidding. With the screws boiling the sea around them and the boat's rudder trying to take them into a violent left turn, *Thresher* seemed to be on the verge of coming apart at the seams. Her superstructure and hull creaked and groaned mightily, like a prehistoric animal in its death throes, its exoskeleton being wrenched apart by some powerful force.

Some of the men wondered if the strain would rip the tail off their vessel, but that was unlikely. It was far more probable that their screws would be pulled close enough to the surface that they would have little bite, not enough force to break the chain or hook or snagged plane.

The enemy would then scramble onto *Thresher*'s decks with explosives and try to blow the hatch covers. Or simply take their time and cut their way in with torches.

Then Captain Millican would issue the command to light off the charges nestled among the torpedoes.

They would have time for only a short prayer.

The resultant explosion would be heard for miles. The sea would burn. Bits of metal and rubber and glass and human beings would fall from the sky like hail for the next several minutes.

And that would be it.

Suddenly *Thresher* lurched downward and swerved around fiercely, sending sailors lurching painfully to the deck. The submarine's tail skewed wildly as those still standing hugged anything solid as hard as they could.

The hook was loose!

However, that meant another bad scenario was now set in motion. They were plunging rapidly toward the shallow bottom. A collision with the seafloor at that speed would certainly do lots of damage and possibly be fatal. Even if they slowed the dive, they would likely burrow into the thick mud down there, maybe deeply enough that they would be trapped.

Instantly blown to bits? Trapped on the bottom of the sea? Trapped at least until the air ran out or they escaped one at a time through the torpedo room hatches, drifting to the surface in their Mae West life vests, directly into the arms of the Japanese?

Neither fate was appealing.

"Blow bow buoyancy! Blow bow buoyancy!" Millican commanded without hesitation. He was still remarkably calm and cool, as if this were little more than a training exercise somewhere off the shores of Oahu and Diamond Head.

Highly compressed air forced water out of the tanks in the heavy forward part of the submarine. They could only hope they could get enough water out to help control the angle and thus the speed of their dive. Men fought with their controls to regain mastery over the freed ship. Then maybe they would be able to swim away to deeper, safer waters.

It seemed they plummeted toward the bottom for an hour, but it was only seconds. They were able to get control of the dive moments before they hit and immediately made a turn for deeper water.

Meanwhile, the enemy realized their trophy fish had found a way to get unhooked. One second their stern was squatted down in the water, bringing in their catch. The next they were bouncing from the freed tension.

They began to chunk depth charges at the submarine.

Below, aboard *Thresher*, the renewed and relentless pounding was nerve-racking, but at least they were free to try to escape.

It was the darkness of night that ultimately came to their rescue. The trail of air bubbles on the surface was no longer visible in the dark tropical sea.

Thresher was finally able to slip away from beneath the enemy vessels that were so close to landing a truly big one.

According to the sonarman's count and the entry made later in the ship's deck log, in less than twelve hours, forty-one depth charges and at least two bombs rocked *Thresher* and her crew. Still, they survived that barrage, as well as the experience of being firmly hooked on the end of a chain fishing line.

Millican was not deterred one whit by the harrowing events. The skipper continued to attack everything he saw that resembled a target as they made their way toward Fremantle-Perth. His crew quickly gained confidence and downright affection for their new skipper. Though they had had those distressing experiences with him at the helm, he had still done exactly what he had told them he would do. He pushed the attack when it was prudent. Yet he did it with the intention of getting his ship and crew to safety afterward.

Official records that credit World War II submarines for ships sunk are notoriously conservative, relying usually on inadequate Japanese data obtained after the surrender. They show only one vessel at forty-eight hundred tons sent to the bottom by *Thresher* on that, her fourth war patrol. Millican and his crew were certain of several others, though. Other worthy targets were lost when dud torpedoes failed to explode.

Still, the best days were ahead for the *Thresher* and "Moke" Millican. And young Charlie Rush would soon be aboard to experience much of it for himself. Along the way, he would get his initial education in submarines, learning how things should be done on the "plunging boats" if they meant to defeat this enemy and go home.

CHAPTER THREE

HOT RUN

"War is hell."

—General William Tecumseh Sherman

C harlie Rush later described Captain "Moke" Millican as "a multitalented genius, a fascinating person. By observing his action in many crises I learned . . . what enabled me to save USS *Billfish* in November 1943."

Rush made three war patrols out of Fremantle, Australia, with Millican and *Thresher*, then two more on *Thresher* after Millican was relieved. When he first joined the crew in Fremantle, he listened to the amazing stories—maybe slightly embellished—of the boat's first trip from Pearl Harbor, including the grapnel incident, which was now legendary among the boats in the Pacific. It would not be long before Rush would experience firsthand other examples of Millican's leadership, courage, and resourcefulness. And those examples would confirm that he was a man to emulate anytime in the future when Rush had the chance.

He remembers that the skipper seemed to always be one move ahead of the enemy, ready for whatever might come his way. His style inspired the crew mightily. That was certainly a change from Rush's previous CO experience on the destroyer. *Thresher*'s crew would follow their captain anywhere.

Millican demonstrated his ingenuity from the very beginning. When he first arrived in Fremantle with *Thresher*—and while Charlie Rush was still trying to make the switch from destroyers to submarines—"Moke" Millican became one of the first members of Admiral Lockwood's "Gun Club."

Charles Lockwood had long advocated arming submarines with larger deck guns for defensive purposes. Shortly after he assumed command of the squadron in Western Australia, Lockwood received several five-inch deck guns that had been stripped from other submarines. They had been previously installed on older boats but they were simply too heavy for them. Those guns were likely bound for the scrap yard or to be installed on surface ships. But that was before Lockwood took possession of them and ordered that they be put on several boats in his new squadron.

Thresher was the second boat to get a big gun. Despite his ideas about the weapons being defensive, Lockwood encouraged Millican and others to use them on offense as well if they so desired.

Millican took his commander's suggestions seriously. He liked the possibilities, considering the submarine's ability to sneak up on a target while submerged, pop to the surface before the enemy knew they were there, go in close with the gun barking, and take down the enemy vessel without wasting a precious torpedo. Besides, such a weapon could well save their lives if they ever found themselves caught on the surface and had to fight their way out of a jam.

On several occasions, Millican made daring surface attacks using his .51-caliber deck gun. That was partly because he felt it was the best way to sink the enemy ship in that particular situation. But it was mostly because the torpedoes used by the American submarine fleet at that time continued to malfunction at an alarming rate.

On Millican's first patrol with the new weapon bolted to her deck—and Charlie Rush's first patrol as her engineer—*Thresher* attacked a three-thousand-ton freighter at the south end of the Makassar Strait. She did it using only the deck gun.

They drove the ship into shallow water and she probably sank there. Unfortunately, though, the captured Japanese records would not confirm it after the war, so *Thresher* received no credit for the unusual accomplishment.

No matter. Millican and his pleased squadron commander, Admiral Lockwood, claimed the largest ship sunk to that point in the war solely by the use of a deck gun. Millican was rapidly heading for legendary status, right along with the other submarine "aces."

On the day after Christmas 1942, *Thresher* was patrolling a sealane between Surabaya and the main Japanese base in Singapore. At midafternoon, as they made regular stops to raise the periscope and look around, the watch officer spotted smoke on the horizon. The smoke almost certainly signaled a ship, steaming along and ripe for the taking. Any ship was a potential target. Millican ordered them to the surface so they could move more quickly to a point where they could intercept, observe, and possibly attack.

While submerged, the World War II–era submarine could travel only about eight or nine knots, and even then only for short periods of time or they risked using up all their battery power. They also had to come to an almost complete stop to use the periscope. On the surface, though, they could make as much as twenty knots and were almost as seaworthy as many surface vessels.

Even so, this ship was moving faster than that and there was a good chance she was about to slip away. *Thresher* had to do some maneuvering to flank the target ship, which was zigzagging specifically to try to avoid a submarine attack. That alone confirmed for Millican that this was a worthy target. If she was worried enough about a submarine attack to zig and zag, she carried something valuable enough for him to take the time and effort to sink her.

Thresher finally drew close enough to see the ship's masts and line up for an attack. Darkness was about to fall.

In the conning tower, Millican peered through the optics of the periscope at the ship they had run down. There was a smile on his face. Easy pickings. There was no way they could miss bagging this game.

He gave the command to fire the torpedoes.

Thresher fired three torpedoes at what amounted to point-blank range. They waited for the flash and fire and boom. The men in the conning tower watched their skipper's face. The flash would often reflect through the periscope on his cheeks. Or his body language and facial expression would tell them how good the hit was.

No explosion. No flash.

"Sonar, you still hear our fish?" Millican asked. "They still running? No way we missed with all three!"

"Captain, I heard two clunks," the sonarman reported. "Two duds."

Millican tried to hide his anger, but all the men on duty in the conning tower saw his aggravation. They wisely kept their heads down.

The target ship steamed on, zigging and zagging, apparently unaware of the close call she had just had. Millican scratched his jaw and pondered his options.

It would not be the only time they had such disappointing results. On the same patrol, *Thresher* had a Japanese submarine—an I-boat—in her sights. Such a chance was rare. It is difficult for one submarine to sink another, since both can move vertically in addition to all the other angles a surface ship can take. That made stalking and shooting much more difficult than lining up and firing on a surface target.

Millican fired two precious torpedoes at the I-boat. One missed and exploded harmlessly on the ocean bottom. The other struck the target squarely against its steel hull, a solid hit, good enough to send her to the bottom.

It failed to explode.

"Damn! We clinked them with a clunk!" Millican told the crew around him. It had become one of the skipper's trademark phrases, but there was very little humor in his voice anymore when he said it.

Millican later complained in his patrol report about those bad fish.

"This command can only feel that there is some deficiency in the performance of the warhead or exploder as only three positive detonations have been heard out of the last fourteen torpedoes fired by this vessel. This belief is confirmed by *positive* [emphasis Millican's] dud hit on target during previous patrol and 3 positive dud hits on derelict during present patrol."

He would not allow his fire control team to take any blame for the lack of detonations, either. He wanted his boss to know that they knew what they were doing, and that the torpedoes they fired carried the latest detonators.

"The firecontrol [sic] party on this vessel have been operating successfully together since shortly after the beginning of the war. Used all large warheads (Mk XIV)."

Such disappointment in the performance of the torpedoes was not an unusual occurrence. The Mark XIV torpedoes experienced several problems. From the very beginning of the war, they tended to run much deeper than set. Despite originally denying it was a problem, the Navy brass and ordnance suppliers finally got to work and fixed that problem. The good submarine skippers had long since figured out how to allow for the anomaly.

But in many cases, the torpedoes still failed to explode, even when they ran where they were supposed to and pounded their noses hard into the side of a target.

Admiral Ralph Christie, the Pacific submarine commander, was a torpedo expert, and he staunchly maintained that there was nothing wrong with the weapons. It was the skippers, he and others insisted, especially the young, brash, impatient skippers, who lacked the makeup to take the time to better line up for an attack. The skippers who had not mastered the fine art of finding the proper position for aiming and shooting them. That was the problem. To that point in the war, and even though they did not agree on much, Charles Lockwood sided with Christie on this one.

"Moke" Millican knew better. He did, after all, hold a master's degree in ordnance engineering from the Naval Academy. However, his research on this particular topic was conducted not in a lab or at the Navy's torpedo test facility at Newport, Rhode Island. He did his experimenting in Japanese-controlled waters, with live torpedoes and all-too-real potential targets. He was convinced the magnetic exploder they were ordered to use on the Mark XIV torpedo was not working correctly and he was quite vocal in his opinions.

But the man who headed up the initial research team that had developed the very same magnetic exploder that Millican and others were labeling as duds?

The holder of his own master's degree in ordnance engineering from the Massachusetts Institute of Technology?

That torpedo expert was none other than Admiral Ralph Waldo Christie.

The lucky target ship "clinked with a clunk" by *Thresher* steamed on that night, but Millican was unwilling to give up so easily. *Thresher* once again raced along on the surface until she was able to catch up to her once again.

The supply of torpedoes—bad or not—was running low, so this time, they fired only two fish, again at close, dead-to-rights distance, in a daring surface attack, doing everything possible to enhance the likelihood of a successful assault.

Again, no blasts.

No flashes on the skipper's face as he stared at the target from the bridge through his binoculars, wincing in frustration.

One torpedo simply missed. The other hit the hull of the target, again with the solid thud of metal against metal, clearly heard and noted by the sonarman. That one torpedo should have been enough ordnance—striking the perfect spot on the hull—to do severe damage. More than enough to send the zigzagging freighter to the bottom.

There was no explosion, though. *Thresher*'s skipper was even more furious this time as he watched the freighter steam benignly away, swerving left and right, seemingly still unaware of her good fortune.

Hell, she did not have to take evasive action. *Thresher* apparently had no torpedo aboard that could sink even a rowboat!

Okay, if the torpedoes were worthless, the captain had an alternate plan.

"Gun crew! Man the deck gun!" Millican barked, the aggravation obvious in his quick, clipped command.

It took the gun crew only three minutes to get into position and make the weapon ready to fire. There was one problem. It was by then a dark, moonless tropical night. The pointer and the trainer, the two men who actually aimed the deck gun, could not see the surface ship very well as she steamed away into the inky blackness. Though powerful and accurate, the gun lacked optical sights.

"Captain, the men can't see where to aim."

It was Charlie Rush who reported the problem to their fuming captain. As the gunnery officer and officer of the deck, it fell to Rush to give the bad news to Millican.

He fully expected the captain to pull back, abandon the attack, submerge, and try one more time with what was left of the torpedoes.

Not "Moke" Millican. He had no intention of allowing the freighter to escape from *Thresher*.

"Have two sets of binoculars sent to the deck," Millican called down the hatch to the men in the conning tower, directly below where he stood on the bridge. Clearly, he was intent on getting this target, no matter what it took. "And some tying cord, too. Twenty feet should do it."

Then the skipper came down from the bridge to where Rush and the gun crew waited on deck, wondering what he was up to.

"Charlie, open the breech," he ordered.

Millican leaned over and, using his own binoculars, sighted through the big gun's barrel until he could make out the target on the darkening horizon.

"Mark!" he called out, and the trainer and pointer each set their own binoculars and tied them to the gun in that exact position. Rush watched the whole thing in amazement. It was a simple solution, but who else would have ever thought of it?

"Ready, Captain," they said, and Millican quickly climbed back up to the bridge.

"Commence firing!" he shouted, as he simultaneously gave the speed and direction commands to the men in the control room to maneuver them closer to the freighter.

The very first shot struck the target amidships. Bright white smoke erupted. The crew figured they had hit a steam boiler. That was escaping steam they were seeing.

However, the enemy ship had spotted the flash from the five-inch gun's muzzle. She turned, clearly intent on ramming *Thresher*. At the same time, the ship's crew began firing machine guns at the submarine. The tracers that accompanied the bullets were already training in on Millican and his boat.

Ignoring the slashes of fire that lit up the sea, the gun crew kept firing, even as Captain Millican turned them around and pulled the submarine quickly out of range of the ship's weapons. Then a shell from the deck gun stopped the machine-gun fire altogether and the enemy vessel abruptly halted its advance.

"She's dead in the water, Captain," Rush reported.

"How many rounds do you have left?" Millican asked.

"We've shot seventy-five. We only have ten rounds left."

"Let's get closer and use that at her waterline," the skipper said.

They did, but that still was not enough to sink the vessel.

"Line up for a stern shot," the captain said.

They fired one of their few remaining torpedoes at the wounded ship. They were close enough that they would easily be able to feel the explosion. Maybe even the heat from the blast.

But yet again, there was no detonation. Unbelievable!

This one, too, was a dud and had failed to explode.

"Captain, she's starting to list," Rush reported. And she was. Men were beginning to jump overboard, too.

Then they figured out what had happened. Since they were so

close when they fired the torpedo—dud or not—it still had enough punch when it struck the target to gouge a big hole in her hull just below the ship's waterline.

Hell, if they could not blow them up, they would just use those otherwise worthless torpedoes to punch holes in their targets. Use them like medieval battering rams!

That finally did it. The vessel heeled over slowly, taking on water through the hole in her side. Then she began to go down quickly. Even in the darkness, they could see survivors continuing to jump from the tilting deck into the sea while others furiously lowered lifeboats.

Millican's stubbornness had finally paid off.

"Charlie, what do you think about picking us up a couple of prisoners of war?" Millican asked his young gunnery officer.

Rush had worked with Millican long enough already to know that if the skipper asked for an opinion, he wanted a straight answer.

"No, sir," Rush answered without even thinking about it. It was a sure bet the freighter had called for help by then. Destroyers with decks full of depth charges were certainly on the way to join the party. "Let's get the hell out of here."

Millican winked and gave orders to "get the hell out of there," sounding the dive Klaxon and taking *Thresher* down quickly until she disappeared beneath the glassy surface of the sea. Only eddies and swirls marked where she had just been.

Sure enough, as they checked behind them one more time through the periscope, they spotted a destroyer approaching the sinking ship at full speed, almost certainly responding to a distress call. They had skedaddled just in time.

On another patrol, Millican, Rush and the crew of *Thresher* narrowly avoided a true catastrophe. This time, it was one partially of their own making. It is not clear what exactly went wrong, but during a drill, the torpedo in tube number one in the forward tor-pedo room was accidentally fired. The problem was that the out-side door to that tube had not yet been opened.

Just as it was designed to do, high-pressure air rushed into the tube to flush the weapon out so its motor would start to spin and send it on its way. The torpedo—all thirty-five hundred pounds of it—rammed hard into the linkage that opened and closed the door to the tube. Its explosive snout, though not yet armed, protruded outside the door, exposed to the intense pressure of the sea.

The torpedo's motor ran hot, too, swelling the body of the weapon, further jamming it tightly in the tube. The motor finally overheated and stopped, but six hundred pounds of highly explo-sive material still protruded from the submarine. If it blew, *Thresher* would be mortally wounded.

"Hot run, tube one!" came the call from the control room. The words sent chills up the spine of every man aboard who heard them. The ones who were off watch and asleep and did not hear it knew all about it in moments.

"Moke" Millican was having a meal in the wardroom. He was up and running before the ominous announcement on the 1-MC system stopped echoing up and down the length of the boat.

Those men who prayed quietly did so.

There were a total of sixteen ready-to-load-and-launch torpe-does in the forward torpedo room—six inside the tubes, set to go, and ten in heavy storage racks along the sides and under the deck plates. They stood ready to be fired from the six tubes that domi-nated the forward end of the room. Equipment for handling the torpedoes was located there as well. That was some chore, since each torpedo weighed more than a ton and a half.

They were equally dangerous to crew members because of their weight as for their explosiveness. If a torpedo broke loose from its rack or came loose from the chain fall or winch in heavy seas or during an attack, it could injure or kill the men around it. Because they were not armed until they were fired, there was not as much danger from one of them exploding, but if one became lodged in a tube—as happened aboard *Thresher*—it could arm itself and possibly detonate. That could have caused major—and probably catastrophic—damage.

There were other hazards in the forward torpedo room, too. If the boat rammed another vessel or hit a submerged obstruction, it would likely be the first compartment to flood. The tubes themselves were protected from the sea only by doors that covered them when they were not in use.

For that reason, the watertight door that closed the doorway to the compartment behind them was usually locked when they were at battle stations. A flood in the forward torpedo room could not be allowed to spread to the whole ship. Those men trapped there would simply have to sacrifice their lives for their shipmates.

There was also bunk space there for the torpedomen to sleep when they were off duty. Some of the crew's bunks were hung above and below the stacked torpedoes, others were suspended from the overhead, and the rest were on the starboard side, in the torpedo-loading pit. Regardless of where the men slept in this compartment, huge, heavy, deadly torpedoes surrounded them the whole time.

The possibility of having to evacuate the sub in an undersea emergency was always on the minds of the crew members. Here, in the forward torpedo room, there was an escape hatch that the men could open, crawl into, and then flood with seawater. That gave them a last-resort way out of a doomed vessel.

There would typically be a supply of Momsen lungs stored here, too. Those were a rudimentary device that could be strapped on in the event the boat had to be evacuated while it was still submerged. They could be used for breathing while rising slowly to the surface. They were not a perfect solution, and the depth at which they could be effectively used was limited, but they were about the only hope sub sailors had if their boat should be damaged or disabled while submerged.

"All stop! Prepare to surface!" Millican shouted as he made the several steps to the control room, but the command had already been made by the officer of the deck (OOD). Sure enough, the boat was already gliding to a stop. Air was roaring into the tanks and they were starting to head upward.

What were the odds this, too, was a dud torpedo? If it was, it might be a lucky break for a change. If it was not, it could be disastrous.

Millican did not slow down. He was up the ladder and into the conning tower in a second, ready to take a look through the periscope. He could only hope for an empty sea and sky above them. No matter. If the entire Imperial Japanese Navy were waterskiing up there, they had little choice but to surface and take care of the hot run.

There were many possibilities to consider, and most of them were bad. Any forward motion of the submarine might cause the jammed torpedo to arm itself. Then any magnetic hiccup could set it off.

They could not dive because the increased water pressure might cause the inner torpedo tube door to rupture. That would flood the boat and quite possibly sink her. At best, it would leave them with a flooded and locked-off torpedo room, severely hobbled a long way from friendly sanctuary.

Finally, they were in truly dangerous waters. An aircraft, a patrol boat, or a destroyer could catch them on the surface while they tried to free the torpedo. They would either have to dive with a live torpedo stuck out the tube door or risk getting sunk by the enemy on the surface. There was no correct guess there.

"Let's stay at periscope depth until dark," Millican finally decided. "If the thing has not blown up yet, maybe it won't." He looked over at his XO, Bill Post. "Let's pray that thing is another one of Admiral Christie's duds. Maybe it's our luck it has a bad detonator, too."

William Schuyler Post was another officer who proudly learned how to run a boat under "Moke" Millican. Post's career had a black mark on it when he came to *Thresher*. While XO on his first boat, early in the war, he had openly questioned his skipper's conservative tactics, some of which had almost gotten them sunk. Then, on one occasion when the old-school captain remained deep, tracking good targets on sonar but pointedly refusing to stage an attack, Post sarcastically asked him, "Don't you think we ought to at least put up a periscope and take a look?"

It was not the first time Post had embarrassed his skipper with his remarks, and the man used that one question as an excuse to write a letter to his squadron commander recommending that Post be "surfaced," or disqualified from submarines. He was transferred instead to a staff position. Soon, though, he was back on the boats, this time as "Moke" Millican's exec.

"I learned everything I know from him," Post later wrote. "He had a TDC [torpedo data computer] in his head. He was a scrapper. He knew what he was doing."

Post, the submarine officer who was almost sent home for pressing his captain to act, went on to successfully captain USS *Gudgeon* (SS-211) and USS *Spot* (SS-413), putting the latter boat into commission in August 1944. His style in both commands was quite similar to Millican's.

Thresher surfaced as soon as dusk settled over the ocean, the torpedo still a ticking time bomb in the forward tube. The sea was calm and there was nobody else—friend or foe—in sight. Truth was, even an ally was not necessarily a good thing to encounter out there. Such an unexpected meeting could be just as fatal as a meet-up with the enemy.

The lookouts nervously scanned the horizon, trying not to glance down at the bow of the ship, where the hot run was. The radar operator kept an eye on his scope, half holding his breath, while a man with a diving mask hurriedly went over the side to try to see if he could tell how much damage there was.

As it turned out, he could not see much at all in the darkness. But Millican had another idea.

"OOD, let's see how high we can make the bow of this sewer pipe float. Flood the stern tanks and blow the bow tanks."

Number one tube is the uppermost of the three that are aligned from top to bottom on that side of the submarine. They might be able to rock the boat back on its rear end by flooding the tanks back there. Then they could get the damaged door out of the water enough for a look and possibly a fix.

While they could not quite manage to get it high and dry, they were still able to get enough of the tube door out of the water so they could open the inner door without completely flooding the torpedo room.

Then they rigged a chain fall—a winchlike device—and attached it to the heavy weapon from the inside. With an all-out effort from the strongest men in the crew, they managed to drag the torpedo back down the tube and then hoisted it out into the compartment. They carefully slid it backward until all its weight was on its rack. Then they reclosed the inner torpedo tube door.

Finally, *Thresher* would be able to dive if she needed to, but there was a snag. She could not safely go very deep. The outer door, damaged by the hot run, was still jammed open to the sea. High water pressure at much beyond two hundred feet deep could still cause flooding in the compartment.

Millican took the boat down to get them off the surface and to seek a calmer place for what had to happen next.

That would be disarming the fish by removing the damaged detonator. Everyone got the order to evacuate the torpedo room and they reluctantly did. The watertight door into the hallway that ran the length of the boat was closed and locked. Two brave torpedomen remained behind, just the two of them in the compartment.

Their job was a particularly precarious one, but something they had trained to do many, many times. They were to remove the exploder from inside the damaged torpedo, and do it without setting the deadly thing off. There was no way to know if the detonator was damaged by the contact with the outside tube door, ready to blow at a touch. Not until they got the screws out and took a look.

If the torpedo exploded, many on the boat would be injured or killed. Even if only the exploder blew, the two torpedomen would be in seriously grave danger, but the ship would be saved. So they had to separate exploder from torpedo as quickly and safely as they could.

It was a tense time. The men, their hands wet with perspiration, slowly and carefully pulled the exploder from the weapon. When it was finally loose, they cautiously lifted it from where it nested inside the torpedo.

Thresher was now safe. But the torpedomen's ordeal was not yet over.

Both sailors held on to the exploder tightly, just in case the other sneezed or lost his grip with his sweaty hands.

They could not relax yet. Any kind of unexpected current that caused the boat to shift suddenly could also make them lose their balance and drop the dreaded thing onto the deck.

One of the men then cradled the device to his chest, holding tightly with both arms. The torpedoman, his clothing soaked with sweat, seawater, and oil, the exploder mechanism hugged to his chest with both burly arms, made his way over to the ladder that led up to the escape hatch that opened onto the deck outside.

The captain had brought the boat gently back to the surface as soon as he got word that the men had successfully extracted the exploder. Gingerly carrying his volatile package held close to his body with one hand, the torpedoman carefully climbed up the ladder using his free hand to hold on to the rungs. He hoped he could maintain his grip with his wet fingers. His buddy followed closely, ready to catch his shipmate or his parcel should he slip or drop it. Once topside, the men walked cautiously across the slick, wet surface of the deck. They slowly made their way over to the edge.

It was a warm night, the sky filled with stars but, luckily, no moon. However, the torpedomen did not pause to admire the tropical evening. With a big heave, the one with the exploder in his hands tossed it as far from the boat as he could send it. Then he braced himself for any possible explosion.

Once again, there was none. This time no blast was a good thing.

"Moke" Millican had made all the right moves. The crew had performed flawlessly during the "hot run," one of the most dreaded occurrences on any submarine.

And a young submarine officer named Charlie Rush had taken note of both. He had never been prouder of a skipper or a crew than he was at that moment.

Rush went on to make a total of three submarine war patrols on *Thresher* with "Moke" Millican in command. Then he made two more runs as a member of the wardroom crew under Lieutenant Commander Harry Hull. However, even after the first run with Millican, he was more convinced than ever that he had made the right choice in moving from surface ships to the diesel boats. Here, he was making a difference in the war almost every day. He continued to be impressed with the caliber of men who volunteered to man and command these stealthy vessels.

Admiral Charles Lockwood was equally taken with Millican and his crew. He began dictating that his most promising prospective commanding officers go out on patrol with Millican so they could see firsthand how a submarine should operate, and how a skipper should run his boat.

Lockwood wrote to his commanding officer, "He [Millican] is really a remarkable type, and I wish I had a couple dozen more like him."

Others did not agree.

When "Moke" Millican returned to Australia from his fourth patrol at the helm of *Thresher*, he complained once again to his superiors about the failure rate of the Mark XIV torpedoes. The duds were putting boats and crews in jeopardy and were seriously hampering the submarines in their attempt to cut the Japanese supply lifelines.

Millican and most of his fellow submarine captains and their fire control parties were competent and able to fire the weapons accurately. They were hitting their targets consistently. The torpedoes simply did not explode when they did.

The failure was in the detonator. Ralph Christie's detonator.

That fact did not deter Millican's efforts to let his superiors know his opinion. When his complaints ended up in a written report submitted by one of the skipper's superiors, Admiral Christie was livid. He was tired of the griping, and especially from the skippers in his own squadron, like Millican. The detonators worked as they were supposed to if the skippers fired them at the recommended angle.

"There is to be no wrangling in print about torpedoes," he ordered bluntly. "The torpedoes are fine."

Whether it was his opinions about the torpedoes that caused it or not, "Moke" Millican was summarily sent back to the States for what was described as rest and relaxation—R & R—even though he maintained that he was fit and ready to take *Thresher* back out for another run.

It was not to be.

After that involuntary leave, Millican's orders sent him to take over command of USS *Escolar* (SS-294), a new submarine then under construction at Cramp Shipyards in Philadelphia.

It was to be an ill-fated assignment.

In September 1944, with Millican in command, *Escolar* was part of a wolf pack known as "Millican's Marauders," operating in the Yellow Sea, between Korea and China and not far from the Japanese Home Islands. On September 30, one of the other boats in the pack received a message from Millican that he and the crew were having a spirited fight with another vessel. Reading between the lines in the dispatch, it appeared the aggressive skipper was having a good time out there. In true Millican fashion, he was using his deck gun in the engagement, just as he had with *Thresher*.

Escolar routinely reported her position a few days later to one of the other boats in the wolf pack, USS *Perch* (SS-313). From that point on, she missed all of her other scheduled check-ins.

No one ever heard from Millican and *Escolar* again.

The new submarine and her crew were officially declared lost when they did not return to port at Midway on the expected date,

November 13, 1944. Naval records indicate that the most likely cause of her loss was that she hit a mine.

That may have been the case, but it was a well-known fact that most of the submarines built at the Cramp Shipyards had mechanical and structural problems. There is a possibility that *Escolar* was lost to something other than enemy fire or a mine blast, but we will likely never know for sure.

She was the forty-first of fifty-two submarines lost in World War II. Her crew is listed among the approximately thirty-six hundred submariners who died in the war.

William John "Moke" Millican received two Navy Crosses for his actions as captain of *Thresher* during his four patrols at her helm, both awarded while he was still her commander. The Navy Cross is the highest award that can be issued by the Department of the Navy and is second in stature only to the Congressional Medal of Honor. The citations noted that the awards went to Millican for "gallantry and intrepidity," and for "extraordinary heroism and distinguished service." Both citations also read, "His conduct throughout was an inspiration to his officers and men and in keeping with the highest traditions of the United States Naval Service."

There is no point in speculating about what might have been, and especially in the chaos of war. If Millican had been allowed to continue to serve as captain of *Thresher*, would he have survived the war? We will, of course, never know.

Did petty differences over the effectiveness of the torpedoes lead to Millican's reassignment and, ultimately, his death? Or, as was typical, was the prescribed trip home and the assignment to new construction destined to happen regardless, even if there had not been the issue of his being so vocal with his opinions about the torpedoes?

Did Millican's daring combat tactics finally get him and his boat into a situation they could not get out of?

Again, we will likely never know.

Today, one of the primary athletic fields at Pearl Harbor, Hawaii, bears the name Millican Field in his honor.

USS *Thresher* ultimately completed fifteen war patrols. Decommissioned in July 1946, her service to her country completed, the submarine was, like so many of her sisters, eventually sold for scrap in 1948.

Another ship named *Thresher* plays an especially tragic role in submarine history. The second *Thresher* (SSN-593) was the lead boat in a new class of nuclear-powered vessels. While still undergoing sea trials on April 9, 1963, she went down, almost certainly due to mechanical problems, about two hundred miles east of Cape Cod.

A hundred and twenty-nine men died—crew members, other representatives of the military, and civilian technicians—making it the deadliest submarine accident in U.S. Navy history. Her loss led to the development of the Navy's sub-safe program, which has been a big factor in preventing any other accidents of that magnitude since.

CHAPTER FOUR

TOOTHACHES AND STETHOSCOPES

"War is fear cloaked in courage."

—General William Westmoreland

L ieutenant Charlie Rush had himself one monstrous tooth-
ache.

After five submarine war patrols on *Thresher*, he returned to Fremantle with a mouthful of trouble — a couple of badly
infected wisdom teeth. He had not seen a doctor or dentist in almost two years, since leaving the Naval Academy. The Navy dentist
he consulted told him that the situation was potentially life threat-
ening. He was not to go back out on patrol until the sulfa drugs had
the infection under control and the teeth were yanked.

The irony that bad teeth might do the job the Japanese had so
far failed to do was not lost on Rush. Still, he was disappointed that
his dental problems had interrupted his time aboard *Thresher* or
kept him off whatever his next boat would have been.

It all worked out, though, when he recovered from the bad
choppers and quickly drew an interesting assignment. The Navy
put him in charge of relief crews for all the submarines operating
out of that port. When a boat came in from patrol, Rush and his
team assessed what personnel needs the skipper and his officers
had before the vessel returned to the war. He kept track of which

enginemen, electricians, torpedomen, officers, and other key crew members might be available for reassignment, as well as newly trained recruits who showed up, ready to go to work.

It was a crucial job. The goal was to get the right recipe of experienced men—especially in the more critical roles—and mix in the green newcomers so the crew would mesh. If the proper makeup was reached, the experienced sub sailors could help train newcomers so they could effectively gain experience and ultimately train and relieve the next batch, all while sinking enemy ships and making it back to port safely after the run.

Rush enjoyed the duty very much, even if he did often wish that he could rejoin his shipmates on *Thresher* or another boat. Still, he knew what was going on out there and was well aware that shore duty was not necessarily a bad thing. It gave him the opportunity to work with all the skippers, execs, and other officers, to get to know them. That could only help him when he did go back to a boat, and later in his Navy career, too. Besides, even if he was not launching torpedoes, diving the boat, or blasting away with Millican's deck gun, he was performing a vital role in helping to win the war.

There was the fact that he had a girlfriend in Fremantle whom he liked very much, too, and he could now be with her almost every night, not waving good-bye to her from the bridge of a submarine as she watched from the pier. The Australians were a warm people anyway and were most appreciative of what the Americans were doing for their country. They recognized that the American presence was a factor in Japan's not invading their country. Fremantle and Perth were wonderful places to recuperate from the rigors of the war, and the Aussies made certain that the submarine crews and support staff wanted for nothing.

It was, quite frankly, good duty.

Meanwhile, a new submarine, USS *Billfish*, was just completing her first war patrol under the command of Lieutenant Commander Frederic Lucas. She was plying the waters of the Indian Ocean, on her way back to the Squadron Sixteen headquarters in Western Australia. *Billfish* was one of a new breed of submarines—the *Balao* class—which featured a thicker hull, greater range, the newest radar, and other capabilities that made her arguably the most advanced warship in history. She was about 312 feet long, could make just over twenty knots on the surface and about ten knots when submerged, and typically carried a crew of sixty-six men. She boasted ten twenty-one-inch torpedo tubes, six forward and four aft, and usually had twenty-four torpedoes aboard when she departed on patrol.

"Test depth," the deepest point to which the submarine could safely go, was listed as 412 feet. Beyond that, the crushing pressure of the sea would begin to deform the thick steel hull and wreak all sorts of havoc on the boat's plumbing, if not the nerves of her crew. Still, unlike her predecessors, this class of submarine could achieve a "crush depth"—the point at which water pressure would likely cause the hull to begin to fail—of more than six hundred feet.

When leaving on patrol, their fuel tanks were filled with heavy diesel fuel. No fuel tank was allowed to have air in it. If it did, the tank would collapse if submerged very deep. The diesel fuel, which was lighter than seawater, was drawn off from the top of a fuel tank and burned by the engines. The heavier seawater was pumped in to compensate so that the fuel tanks were kept full of liquid at all times.

Also, when the boats left port on a patrol, every nook and cranny was filled with provisions for the run. Even the decks were covered with cans of food, and the crew literally had to walk around on their groceries until they were used up. That, too, had to be calculated and tracked. If the boat became too heavy on one side or one end, it could make a dive or surface an even more challenging adventure than it was already.

Oddly, even though they were built to run on and under the sea, water was a precious commodity aboard submarines. Seawater could not be used in the storage batteries, of course. Only distilled water was pure enough for that purpose. Submarines carried distilling systems that converted seawater to pure, clean distilled water.

The old joke among submariners was that if the distilled water was pure enough, they used it in the batteries. If it was not, they used it for drinking and cooking. That joke was not far-fetched at all.

Notice no mention of water for laundry or bathing. A shower aboard a submarine was a rare luxury. It was far more common for the crew to grab a quick bath while running through a rainstorm than to be able to take much more than a spit bath. In reality, when leaving port, the enlisted men's double shower stalls were usually crammed full of potatoes and other stores. They would not use them for their intended purpose anytime soon—if at all—after heading out on patrol.

Another old joke was that showers were not necessary. That nobody noticed body odor aboard the boats. The diesel fumes and battery acid and other assorted aromas pretty well took care of covering that up.

Like her sisters, *Billfish* sported four huge diesel engines, very similar to those that propelled locomotives. These engines, contained in two engine rooms with one on each side of the boat in each compartment, did not directly drive the screws. They hooked instead to a high-powered electrical generator. Output from the generators created power to operate electrical motors in the motor room when the boat was on the surface, as well as powering the ship's electrical systems. While on the surface, the generators charged the batteries, which supplied power—for a limited time—to run the electric motors while the submarine was submerged. These batteries were located in compartments beneath the main deck, one below the crew quarters and the other forward, beneath the officers' quarters and wardroom.

World War II American fleet submarines—like *Billfish*—had two batteries, each composed of 126 cells. Each cell was about fifty-four inches high, over a foot deep, and almost two feet wide, and weighed about 1,650 pounds. As the cells were being charged, they produced explosive hydrogen gas, which had to be removed through the ventilation system and discharged outside the pressure hull. Meters were hung throughout the vessel to keep tabs on the accumulation of the gas inside the boat. It was a definite and perpetually present explosion hazard.

Another potential problem with the batteries was saltwater contamination. If salt water mixed with the electrolyte, poisonous chlorine gas could be produced. That, if concentrated enough, was an obvious danger to the crew.

Because of the exhaust gases and smoke and the need for plenty of air for the diesel engines to run, they could not operate while the boat was submerged. Even if some sort of snorkel system made it possible to run the engines, pulling in air and venting smoke—such a snorkel was actually employed in some submarines after World War II—they still made plenty of noise and black smoke, making detection by surface craft easy.

If the boat ran at her full eight to ten knots' speed that was available while submerged, a full charge on the batteries allowed only about an hour's worth of power. Those same batteries also supplied the juice for air-conditioning and air scrubbing as well as all other electrical systems while submerged, too. The only way to recharge them was to surface and fire up the diesel engines. There was the crew's dilemma.

Only battery power could be used while submerged, and batteries could not be charged while underwater. The submarine had to remain on the surface while charging, and that could take a while to get a full charge. Being submerged with little or no battery power remaining could be catastrophic. That was only one thing a sub crew had to watch continually and calculate accurately so as not to run out of juice.

Frederic Lucas was a plank owner on *Billfish*. That means he was a member of the crew that put her into commission. Another submariner standing at attention on the deck of *Billfish* on April 20, 1943, for the official commissioning ceremony—and thus another plank owner—was an experienced submariner named C. T. Odom, a "rag hat," or enlisted man.

Charley Odom joined the Navy the first time in 1934 and selected submarine duty, primarily because he wanted to learn more about diesel mechanics. Many who enlist and choose submarine service will admit they did so because of the training they got in specialized areas. Odom went to USS *S-1* (SS-105), another of the primitive submarines built during and just after World War I. It was there he learned how to properly maintain diesel engines, and he learned well.

Odom decided he wanted to return to civilian life after a six-year hitch. He left the Navy in 1940 and went to work at the DuPont explosives factory in Memphis, Tennessee, keeping the locomotives in the plant's roundhouse running. The plant had one major customer for its powder and shipped most of it there. Great Britain needed all they could get to fend off the attacks from Nazi Germany, but not all of it made the transit across the Atlantic. The German U-boats saw to that.

When the United States finally entered the war after Pearl Harbor, Odom was among the first in line to re-up. He knew he had some skills that would be very much in demand. So even though he had just married an Army nurse and settled into home life, he rejoined and went back to sea.

He returned to the Navy in early 1942 as a chief petty officer—an "old chief" at the age of twenty-nine. He was soon a part of the commissioning crew of the newly constructed submarine, helping put *Billfish* through her sea trials, getting her and a relatively inexperienced crew ready for war.

His job as chief motor machinist's mate put him in charge of the engine rooms and the twenty or so men who worked there. He had to make certain that the four two-thousand-horsepower diesel engines worked properly and were tuned and ready to go when called upon. That meant regular maintenance, inventorying replacement parts, and sometimes having to repair them in the midst of very trying circumstances.

To the amusement of his gang, Odom often wore a doctor's stethoscope around his neck. Even though the roar of the engines eventually rendered hard of hearing most men who worked in submarine engine rooms, Odom claimed he could tell if one of his engines had a problem just by listening to it through the stethoscope. It was like a physician listening for a heart murmur in his patient's chest.

Crew members made fun of him—behind his back, of course—when he bent over one of the big motors, the stethoscope pressed to its throbbing pulse. They stopped laughing, though, when he diagnosed a small problem before it became a big one, or he was able to quickly locate and fix a glitch before any of them even knew one existed.

Whether it was the stethoscope or not, Odom was a genius when it came to keeping those engines going.

Billfish completed sea trials and training and passed through the Panama Canal in the summer of 1943. When they first entered the Pacific Ocean, she dived for a particular exercise. Some practice depth charges were dropped about a mile away from their position in order to give the crew an opportunity to experience what an attack sounded and felt like.

Not so bad, they thought. Not so bad at least from a mile away.

She and her crew arrived in Australia in early August 1943. After refitting, repairing some things that had broken during the transit, loading on stores, and doing some more chores to get ready, she departed on her first war patrol twelve days later. The run ended on October 10 in Fremantle, the port for Perth.

Captain Lucas ran the patrol the way the Navy taught him to. He was to avoid detection, protect the submarine and crew, and attack if a target presented itself, but only if there was a reasonable chance of success. Then quickly run and hide to avoid enemy destroyers or aircraft. It was crucial that they use the vessel's stealth capabilities to ensure she lived to fight another day.

Minimal risks. No foolhardy attacks. Do not waste torpedoes on long shots. Save them for prime targets when circumstances allowed for a high-probability assault.

Remain silent. Stay hidden. Do not let the enemy know you are in the area. Best to remain hidden and wait for the best targets.

A highlight of *Billfish*'s first run was what was termed an "assist" to another Fremantle boat, USS *Bowfin* (SS-287), a submarine launched one year to the day after the attack on Pearl Harbor. For

TOOTHACHES AND STETHOSCOPES

that reason, she carried the nickname "the Pearl Harbor Avenger." She certainly lived up to her moniker, becoming one of the more productive boats of World War II. She ranks fifteenth among all submarines for number of enemy vessels sunk in the war, even after postwar analysis took away many of her "certain" kills.

Billfish and *Bowfin* were the first two submarines to be assigned as part of the new Squadron Sixteen in Fremantle, so it was only natural that they worked together on their first patrol assignment in the same region of the South China Sea.

Billfish and Lucas hooked up with *Bowfin* and her skipper, Joe Willingham, about a month into the patrol—September 24, in the South China Sea off Indochina, right in the midst of one of Japan's primary shipping lanes—and they began an informal partnership, looking for what intelligence promised them would be a convoy heading their way. Willingham had already become an "ace," having won two Navy Crosses for his actions so far in the war.

The intel proved to be accurate. The convoy was exactly where it was supposed to be the next day. Willingham and *Bowfin* went on to sink half the six-ship convoy, partly using the recently developed and greatly improved torpedo data computer (TDC), but also relying heavily on Willingham's experience, instinct, and best guesses. The attacks were vintage Willingham, similar to the way "Moke" Millican worked.

Willingham described the attack on one of the ships in fascinating detail.

"Commenced swinging to bring the stern tubes to bear on the last ship in this line while watching the hits. The second torpedo fired hit KANO MARU under the bridge, the third hit abaft the mainmast and the after end of the ship burst into flame with explosive violence and burned furiously, the fourth hit abaft the stack, the exact location could not be determined because of the fire. The sixth torpedo was seen to hit the transport slightly abaft the stack while the debris from the fifth was still in the air."

Meanwhile, in his deck logs aboard *Billfish*, Frederic Lucas reported, "Sighted a terrific explosion," and wrote that he saw "fire . . . with dense black smoke" when *Bowfin* hit one of the ships, a tanker. Lucas recorded, "Took photographs. During the next half hour heard and felt 20 explosions believed to be depth charges dropped on BOWFIN. Observed some columns of water in the air during this period."

While *Bowfin* pressed the attack on the convoy, the entries in *Billfish*'s log included a frustrating account of not being able to get into the right position to do anything to help: ". . . another zig of 20 [degrees] away made it impossible to get within firing range of this target either. Tracked the formation submerged watching for BOWFIN to attack." And, "Having attained a position 10,000 yards ahead of target pulled out from track, turned toward, stopped and waited for him. However, two successive zigs away left us with too long a torpedo run, so at 1936 commenced working ahead again."

Lucas finally reached a position where he felt he could prudently attack a stray ship from the convoy. She was one of the vessels that had scattered when Willingham and his crew waded right into the middle of them and blasted the tanker to hell and back. *Billfish* fired five torpedoes from the bow tubes, and then immediatcly went to top speed and headed away from the target. One torpedo hit the target at the stern and the vessel appeared to be dead in the water.

"Intended to run just out of sight and then approach from another bearing, but the target commenced firing a 4" or 5" gun, firing two about 90 [degrees] from our bearing then three in the correct general direction," Lucas wrote.

Lucas kept his vessel at eighteen knots, making no turn back to press the attack, speeding away from the damaged ship. He stopped when he was almost eight miles away and tried to spot the target on radar. *Billfish* eventually gave chase again when Lucas felt it prudent, and stayed at it until early the next morning. Somehow, though, they never managed to get close enough to make another attack on the hobbled ship.

At 0631, *Billfish* secured from battle stations.

On September 29, they saw what they determined to be an unescorted tanker emerging from a rain squall. Lucas fired four torpedoes before the vessel made a sudden turn. That was when he saw she was clearly not a tanker at all. It was a patrol vessel of some type. The torpedoes, set to run at twenty feet deep to punch holes below the waterline of a big tanker full of oil and riding low in the water, ran well beneath the much smaller and lighter patrol ship and did not explode.

Billfish turned and called upon all the power the diesel engines could muster in order to get away. The Japanese patrol craft no doubt knew they were there and would come looking for them.

Lucas could not understand how he and his crew had misidentified the target so badly.

"Three officers viewed the tanker by periscope on first contact . . . whether it was coincidence or a trick that brought us into the contact with the smaller vessel on the same course and at the same speed or whether he was an escort which had joined the tanker, is not known," his report states.

The next several days were spent patrolling near the Hongom Peninsula, near what is now Vietnam, and dodging possible patrol vessels, most of it in monsoon weather. Lucas chose not to engage any of the ships they encountered.

"Since our presence on the coast had not yet been disclosed, avoided and proceeded south," he wrote, justifying the lack of aggressive action on their part.

Then the new boat had one more chance to make her first run a spectacular success. They spotted a small convoy ambling along at only eight or nine knots. Lucas immediately began angling for an attack.

Angling patiently but fruitlessly for more than ten hours.

Finally, at 4:38 in the afternoon, he shot four torpedoes, and then immediately went deep and rigged for a depth-charge attack. On the way down, they heard one of the four torpedoes explode. The sonarman also reported that he heard the screws of one of the ships stop turning.

Fifteen depth charges rattled *Billfish*. The submarine eventually settled at five hundred feet, attempting to hide beneath an area of colder water that might scramble sonar pings from the surface ship. That was one of the tricks submarine skippers quickly learned. The difference in seawater temperature at different depths gave a false reading on sonar of where the pings were coming from when they echoed back.

Three and a half hours after the last depth charge exploded, Lucas brought his boat to the surface and checked for damage. It was light and the crew quickly repaired it. There was no sign of the vessel they believed they had hit. No oil slick, no debris, and no damaged vessel sitting dead in the water.

Billfish received credit for damaging two ships on that first war patrol—a total of 11,860 tons—but sinking none in the process. Still, despite the lack of success on any of the other targets, Admiral Christie was pleased with his experienced captain's first run on his new submarine.

"This patrol is considered successful for purpose of awarding the

Submarine Combat Insignia," Christie wrote in his endorsement, a part of the official patrol report. "The Task Force Commander congratulates the Commanding Officer, Officers, and crew of the BILLFISH upon an 'assist' in the group attack on the convoy on 25 September, and upon inflicting . . . damage on the enemy."

The commander of Task Group Seventy-one Point Three, J. M. Haines, wrote in his endorsement of *Billfish*'s initial run, "It is unfortunate that the attacks on the two convoys were not more productive of visible results."

Still, no one questioned Captain Lucas or his methods. Admiral Christie was especially pleased with the results of the teamwork between Lucas and Willingham. *Billfish* came back in one piece. Now she would get some needed maintenance, give her crew a chance to enjoy the Australian hospitality, and pick up some new crew members as she prepared for her next run.

That was where Lieutenant Charlie Rush's fate became forever entwined with *Billfish*, her skipper, and her crew.

While *Billfish* was tied up at the submarine pier in Fremantle on October 10, 1943, Rush, in his capacity as duty officer, met with the skipper and his new XO, who had come aboard for her second run. Rush evaluated what the boat needed in the way of replacement personnel. He was pleased to see they had a strong CPO running the engine room—Charley Odom—and that would enable him to assign some relatively inexperienced crew members to that department.

The second in command, Gordon Matheson, seemed to be a good submariner, but Rush knew little about him. He was new to *Billfish*, having replaced Frank Selby, an experienced submariner who had been with Lucas on the boat's first patrol as XO.

Selby had been rushed off *Billfish* when she returned from that first patrol and was immediately given his own command of another submarine, USS *Puffer* (SS-268). She was a submarine with some disturbing recent history.

During her just-completed run, the captain and his officers had lost control of their crew during a vicious depth-charge attack in the Makassar Strait. After staging an assault on an enemy vessel, a destroyer chased them deep and began littering the sea with depth charges. *Puffer* would ultimately remain submerged for more than thirty-seven hours, which was easily a record to that point, and probably for the entire war.

During that interminable siege, the strain, the fatigue, the heat, and the foul air contributed to a general loss of morale and fighting will. And, unfortunately, to a failure of command.

At one point, the captain determined that they should surface, man the deck gun, and try to fight their way out of their dire situation. When some of his officers and crewmen objected to such an idea, claiming it would be suicide, the captain pointedly avoided making a command decision. Instead he announced that he would take a vote among the crew about what they should do, and he told them that he would do whatever they determined to be the best course.

It is the only recorded instance of a submarine commander taking a vote among the crew on what action should be taken. It is not the way a naval commander is supposed to make decisions.

Though most of the men admitted they were past caring one way or the other, that they had long since given up, the vote was taken. They stayed there, hovering at five hundred feet, still getting rattled occasionally by charges from the dogged destroyer on the surface above them.

Finally, after a day and a half, there was no choice. The men could no longer breathe. Many were in their bunks, unable or unwilling to answer a call to watch.

The captain, without taking a poll this time, ordered *Puffer* to blow the ballast tanks and surface by the shortest route, at a sharp angle. Only one small craft was close and, back on diesel-engine power, they easily outran it on the surface to get away. Then they headed straight back to Fremantle.

When *Puffer* made it back to squadron headquarters, Admiral Christie actually praised the ship and her commander. In his diary, he wrote, "Strength of character, skill and experience and knowledge, the excellent state of training, all helped to save the ship. This was a brilliant job carried through by guts, determination and the inspired example of the Commanding Officer."

Only after a thorough investigation by the squadron staff did the truth emerge. The captain was relieved of duty and the officers and many of the enlisted crew members were scattered among other boats until a disciplinary hearing could be held. Frank Selby, assuming command of *Puffer* after that incident, had himself a handful—50 percent of his crew were newcomers and the other half had been a part of the discipline issue—but he took the helm and never looked back.

Selby eventually took that problem boat—*Puffer*—on four successful war patrols and ended up as the fifty-first most successful submarine skipper of World War II.

Meanwhile, Charlie Rush was rounding out the relief crew for *Billfish*. If he didn't know much about her new XO, he knew even less about Captain Lucas. He was aware that he was an experienced commander with years of service in peacetime prior to the war, though much of it was from behind a desk and not in the conn. In fact, Lucas had come directly from a staff position to the newly constructed *Billfish* when the war started.

Then there was the fact that he had now taken his boat to war and brought her back safely. That Admiral Christie and the other high-level folks seemed pleased with what he had done on that run. And he seemed to be a cordial enough fellow, if just a bit reserved and aristocratic in demeanor. Nonetheless, Rush did his best to get a good mix of crew members before Lieutenant Commander Lucas took *Billfish* back to war.

Then Rush received an unexpected invitation, one that would dramatically change the course of his life.

The young lieutenant was about to embark on a truly remarkable voyage.

A voyage that would not truly end until sixty years later.

CHAPTER FIVE

THE UPSET ELECTRICIAN'S MATE

"Make up your mind to act decidedly and take the consequences. No good is ever done in this world by hesitation."

—Sir Thomas Huxley

C harley Odom was a self-proclaimed "snipe," the term the men who labored in a submarine's engine rooms proudly tagged on themselves. The rest of the crew took to calling them that, too, mainly because it somehow seemed to fit. It soon became a badge of honor for submarine enginemen, just like skinned knuckles, the aroma of sweat and diesel fumes, and grease and oil in every orifice of the body. Even the girls in the submarine bars at various ports were able to tell the enginemen from other crew members, mostly by their distinctive "cologne."

These were the guys who made the boat go, not just when it wanted to but when it needed to—when it needed to go in a hurry. After the torpedoes spun away from their tubes during a surface attack, the snipes knew what came next. If they stayed around after sending away their fish, they were at risk to get pounded for a while. Sometimes, even if they moved away at all good speed, they still got pounded, but at least they had a better chance of survival if they vacated the immediate area where they launched their attack.

Their diesel engines had to respond on command. To keep them in proper condition to give that response, the snipes willingly crawled into filthy bilges, battery wells, and spaces so hot and un-comfortable no normal man would go there. They did it, though, often carrying tools as big and as heavy as they were. Did it without even giving things time to cool down. The engines themselves heated up to about 150 degrees, and when they ran, they created a noise that measured at over a hundred decibels. Today, when you talk with a submarine engineman who served on the diesel boats, you have to yell to be heard. Their hearing would never be the same after standing watch around those loud, hot engines.

Charley Odom was the "old man" in the *Billfish* engine room. He was twenty-nine years old.

Odom took great delight in overseeing the men who worked for him in the engine room, and especially the younger ones. He had his preferences for the kind of sailor he wanted, if and when he was granted a choice. He picked farm boys when he could, even if their submarine knowledge was spotty, because they typically had expe-rience fixing tractors and other machinery back home. The diesel engines did not pose much of a problem for them.

Others, who did not take to the engines as well as some did, became "gauge watchers," the crew members who kept eyes on the indicators that reported to them how well the engines were performing. They performed that function until Odom and his experienced snipes could get them up to speed with wrenches and hammers. By that time, though, they usually got shipped off to another boat.

He taught his guys other nuances of submarining, too. Things that were not part of the curriculum in the classrooms and on the training boats back at sub school. Not in the manuals either. How-ever, they were things that could possibly save their lives someday.

On their first run, during the vicious depth charging they endured, one of the young sailors stared up toward the top of the pressure hull, awaiting the next blast, while he idly stirred his coffee with a metal spoon. Although the youngster did not notice it, the ringing of his spoon against the inside of his ceramic mug created enough of a noise that the Japanese might well have detected it. That could have been more than enough to allow them to home in closer with their charges.

The bastards needed no help!

Odom pointedly took the spoon from his shipmate and whispered to him, "Stir with your finger or don't stir it at all."

"Silent running" meant complete silence.

While they were in Fremantle after the first run, and when Lieutenant Charlie Rush came aboard to determine needs for replacements, one of the men he conferred with was Charley Odom. Rush knew the chiefs often had a better feel for how the current crew was jelling than the officers did, and especially ones as experienced as Chief Odom. They would be honest in asking for only the men they really needed, too, and not simply issue a wish list.

Odom placed his order and then left the boat to enjoy a few days off, though he and the rest of the engine room crew often had to work a good portion of the time when they were in port. Repair crews did most of the work on the idle submarines, but it was still up to the enginemen to get the engines refitted, tuned, and ready for serious duty once they were back on patrol. Working on a busted motor while on patrol was a dangerous proposition. That was especially true if the boat had to be on the surface at the time.

A few days later, after he completed the reassignment of the relief crew for *Billfish*, Charlie Rush heard a knock on his office door.

"Lieutenant, may I have a word?" the visitor said. "I'm John Rendernick. I'll be part of the relief crew on one of the boats here shortly, as soon as I draw my assignment."

Rush scanned his list. Rendernick was a first-class electrician's mate, and, as he said, he was as yet unassigned.

"Sure. What can I do for you?"

"Sir, I have finished up all my paperwork for chief. I was wondering if you could sign my papers before I get placed on a boat and we ship out. I'd really like to go out as a chief if I could."

Making chief petty officer is the biggest promotion a Navy enlisted man can achieve. Such a promotion carries requirements of time in service, superior evaluation scores, and good results on a battery of exams. There is also a requirement of peer review. A chief petty officer can advance only after review by a selection board of active-duty senior and master chief petty officers. Rendernick had successfully navigated his way through all those strenuous requirements. Now there was just the formality of final promotion.

Still, in Rush's estimation, there was one obstacle, one thing that, according to the paperwork before him, Rendernick had not yet achieved.

"Let me ask you, Mr. Rendernick, have you made a war patrol yet? I don't see . . ."

"No, sir," Rendernick replied, shaking his head. "But I'm about to, I'm sure."

"Well, there are lots of first-class guys out there on war patrol right now who take precedence over you. Your scores and recommendations look good, but I think the guys making the patrols deserve to make chief first. Come back to see me when you get back from your first run and we'll make it formal."

Rendernick gritted his teeth, nodded, saluted, and then turned and left Rush's office.

The young lieutenant could tell the sailor was upset with him. Rush felt bad about what he had done. He hated to deny any deserving man a promotion. But he also knew he had good reason for postponing Rendernick's move up the ladder.

Then Charlie Rush faced another serious and totally unexpected decision. This one would directly affect him and his naval career—and damn near cost him his life.

As he was finishing up the crew assignments for *Billfish*, the skipper and his XO asked Charlie to join them at their hotel for a drink. That was somewhat unusual, but the invite seemed innocent enough. At first, Rush thought they might be about to try to ask for some kind of special favor in regard to their relief crew. On the other hand, he thought, they might want to take issue with one of the new men he had assigned to *Billfish*. He tried to avoid the politics that sometimes crept into the process, but sometimes they caught up with him.

After exchanging pleasantries and talking briefly about the frustrating first run *Billfish* had just completed, Captain Lucas paused, studied the liquid in his glass, and then looked directly at Rush.

"Mr. Rush, I hear good things about you," he said. "You did a fine job getting us a good set of men, too. Gordy and I have a proposition for you."

Gordon Matheson leaned forward and went straight to the reason for the meeting while his captain ordered another Scotch.

"Captain Lucas and I would like for you to ship over to *Billfish* as our chief engineer."

Rush sat back in his chair, surprised by the XO's proposition. He had not expected a job offer when he joined Lucas and Matheson for that drink.

Charlie knew his war patrol days were likely not over, that he would not be assigning relief crews at Fremantle until the war ended. Not as long as the Japanese continued to run rubber and petroleum from the Philippines and Indochina to the Home Islands. Not as long as there were battleships and carriers that flew the Rising Sun flag and threatened Allied ships. There was still too big a demand for practiced submarine officers for him to remain on shore duty much longer, even if his experience thus far consisted of less than a year in the boats. He was a grizzled veteran compared to many who were out there dodging depth charges and launching torpedoes.

There were other considerations that would have to play into his decision. Rush had a girlfriend and they were close. He liked life in Perth and Fremantle. He was doing an important job, too, and obviously doing it well if he had impressed Lucas and Matheson sufficiently enough for them to offer him a spot in the wardroom on their boat.

Rush finally looked from Lucas to Matheson, smiled, and said, "I thank you for your confidence, gentlemen, but I have a pretty important job to do here. Maybe if you still need an engineer after this run . . ."

But they pressed him, refusing to take his "no" as a final answer.

Rush later claimed that he had no idea why he relented and agreed to accept the billet on *Billfish*. The deciding factor probably was that they sincerely seemed to need him and wanted him to sail with them.

He finally agreed to ship over to *Billfish*.

In all, twenty-three new men came aboard *Billfish* for her second war patrol. Of those, twenty had never been to war in a submarine. Their only experience was the training that they received at sub school in Groton.

Of course, their new engineering officer did not even have the benefit of that schooling. But he had learned at the elbow of "Moke" Millican.

Over the next few days, workmen installed a new type of voice radio unit on *Billfish*—equipment especially designed to allow multiple submarines to better coordinate their joint operations in a war zone, a good addition, considering their informal partnership with *Bowfin*—and completed some minor repairs. On a vessel as complicated as a *Balao*-class submarine, there were plenty of things that could and did break. The crew also finished four days of training, still working with *Bowfin*, which had come in about the same time they did and would once again proceed to the same part of the war as they would for her next run.

Meanwhile, Charlie Rush got his orders to *Billfish* and joined the crew in the midst of preparations for her second war patrol. He knew several of his new shipmates already, including his chief motor machinist's mate, Charley Odom, and, of course, the skipper and his executive officer, who had done such a powerful sales pitch on him.

It still took him a few days to get accustomed to the newer submarine, which was only his second boat. She was slightly bigger but much more advanced in her systems than was *Thresher*, even if there were only about two years' difference in their ages.

As he learned the names and jobs of each of his shipmates, Rush quickly noticed that *Billfish* still had no chief electrician's mate. Rush's replacement had not yet filled that job.

On submarines, it is the EM who stands watch in the maneuvering room, the compartment where the switches, rheostats, and other electrical equipment are located that accepts power from the diesel engines and divides it properly to the batteries and electric motors. Or keeps track of the charge on the massive banks of electric cells and doles it out to the electric motors when submerged. Like most jobs on a submarine, it was a crucial one. Lives depended on its being done well.

Then Charlie Rush had a flash of inspiration. He went to the squadron commander's office, which was housed on a submarine tender parked at the wharf in Fremantle harbor. A tender is a ship that carries equipment, parts, tools, and the men who see to the needs of the submarines.

"I want to assign this man to *Billfish*," he told the duty officer there, and handed him a sheet of paper that contained the details on a sailor named John Rendernick. "And one other thing. Promote him to chief."

Billfish left Fremantle on Monday afternoon, November 1, 1943. Her new chief engineer, Charlie Rush, had the watch on the bridge as they pulled away. He enjoyed the warm breeze and clear blue waters of the Indian Ocean.

Rush had mixed emotions. He had forgotten how much he missed the exhilaration of leaving for a patrol, how special it was to see a well-trained crew at their duty stations, efficiently doing so well what they had prepared to do. Still, it had been difficult to kiss his girlfriend good-bye and leave behind the other friends he had made in his short time there.

With any luck, he told her, he would be back before the end of the year. Maybe in time for Christmas.

Or, if luck did not smile on him and his new submarine, he might not.

When they were about ten miles out to sea, Rush sent word below to have someone get John Rendernick from the maneuvering room. So far, Rush had not bumped into his new chief electrician's mate.

"Tell him the boat's engineer wants to see him on the bridge," Rush said.

When Rendernick popped up the ladder from the conning tower and stepped up to the bridge, it took a moment for his eyes to adjust to the brilliant sunlight of a Southern Hemisphere spring. His jaw dropped when he could finally see that it was Charlie Rush standing there grinning at him.

"Good to have you aboard, Rendernick," Rush said with a smile. "Congratulations on making chief."

The EM was so surprised he almost forgot to accept Rush's offered handshake. Still, the look on his face said, "Oh, no! I have to work for this hard-ass?"

Theirs turned out to be a good relationship, one that would culminate six decades later. Less than two weeks after they left behind the shoreline of Australia, Rush and the crew would learn just what a good thing it was to have Rendernick aboard *Billfish*.

And Charlie Rush would always maintain that this impromptu assignment was the best one he ever gave anybody.

CHAPTER SIX

"CAPTAIN, HE'S GOT US!"

"We often give our enemies the means to our own destruction."

—Aesop

1 *November 1943: 1350. Departed Fremantle, Western Australia for Second War Patrol. Proceeding to Exmouth Gulf in company with U.S.S. BOWFIN and U.S.S. PRESTON, conducting training in coordinated attacks and tests of voice radio communications enroute.*

The patrol report, based on deck logs and the captain's notes, is an official document, a detailed account of a submarine's activities throughout its run. It describes by date and time every occurrence the captain deems important, and has comments from the commanders several layers up the chain of command attached in the form of "endorsements."

It is well-known that many ship captains used this prose to make themselves look good or to advance their careers. Others wrote beautifully, sometimes poetically, and their descriptions and thoughts are downright entertaining. The accuracy of their entries, on the other hand, is sometimes suspect. What is left out could often make a huge difference in determining how successful the patrol was as well as what kind of job the captain and crew—and the ship in general—did on the run.

Frederic Lucas did not embellish much in his patrol reports. His writing was direct, with only an occasional note on why he decided to do certain things the way he did. Now, based on the memories of key crew members, we know he omitted much information about some of the events that occurred during his tenure as skipper aboard *Billfish*. That especially pertains to occurrences during her second war patrol in November and December of 1943.

Out of port and bound for the same coastal waters off Indochina she had worked in on her first run and with a fifty-square-mile patch of ocean to patrol, *Billfish* would first need to thread once again a couple of very hazardous needles along the way.

Lombok Strait connects the Java Sea with the Indian Ocean and is a primary exchange point for the waters of the Indian and Pacific oceans. That creates swift currents, which can be tricky for surface or submerged ships. However, the passage is much deeper—over eight hundred feet deep—than other fingers of water between the long, curved string of islands that make up the southern part of Indonesia. Despite the currents, that makes it a favorite route for ships that draw deep water or desire to have the option of remaining submerged.

Since the Japanese had artillery pieces trained on the strait from both sides, it would have made sense for submarines to make the nearly forty-mile run underwater and out of sight. The problem with that plan was that a submerged vessel, heavy with seawater to keep her from trying to float to the surface, was hard to handle in the currents rushing between the two great oceans. If the moon was new, or if clouds shielded it, the skippers almost unanimously risked a surface passage.

The second needle to thread, Makassar Strait, is a passage between the islands of Borneo and Celebes (now called Sulawesi) in

Indonesia. This strait allows ships to move between the Java Sea to the south, across the equator, and into the Celebes Sea to the north. Despite the Japanese controlling both islands, the strait became a favorite route for submarines traveling between Western Australia and the South China Sea, by a path that took them west of the Philippine Islands, because it took several days fewer than other ways did.

Out of Fremantle, Captain Frederic Lucas directed *Billfish* up the coast of Australia to a point on a peninsula on the continent's far northwest corner, the tiny port town of Exmouth. There, a naval base with the colorful code name "Potshot" had been built specifically to replenish submarines on their way to and from war patrols. It was there that *Billfish* topped off her big diesel fuel tanks—almost ninety thousand gallons of fuel—and added all the provisions the crew could store aboard their boat. They literally walked around on cans of vegetables that they stacked on the decks. The showers—rarely used because of the scarcity of freshwater for such nonessential purposes as bathing or shaving—overflowed with sacks of potatoes and other stores.

From Exmouth, Lucas pointed the bow of his submarine almost due northward, toward Lombok Strait and Makassar Strait beyond. She separated then from *Bowfin* with the intention of hooking up once again in the South China Sea and resuming their informal wolf pack operation. They had their patrol area assigned and their orders were clear. They were to search for convoys that carried oil and rubber from Malaysia to Japan. If they encountered military targets—including troopships—they were to shoot to kill as well, but their primary quarry would be merchant and cargo ships: freighters, tankers, and the like.

As was the practice, along the way they surfaced when it was relatively safe to do so and received constant radio updates on enemy shipping they might encounter along their transit to their patrol box. This included surprisingly good intelligence about convoys—how many ships, what type, and what sort of escort protection they had. Standing orders were to sink anything that they determined to be an enemy vessel, regardless of type or size, and even if it meant they had to deviate from their course toward the South China Sea in order to do so.

However, they also needed to be aware of ships and patrol planes that were specifically looking for American submarines. The toll the Japanese were taking on the U.S. boats was already considerable.

In a classic example of the hunter becoming the hunted, the submarine service was well on its way to racking up the highest casualty rate of any branch of the service anywhere in the war.

9 November 1943: 0330. Moonset. Entered Lombok Strait at 18 knots.

0451. Submerged in Lombok Strait in position 8-30S; 115-49E.

1851. Surfaced and headed north into Macassar [sic] Strait at 14 knots.

Despite the big guns trained on the strait from each side, Lucas decided to make the run through Lombok on the surface. He waited for the slight sliver of moon to set behind the mountainous island to their port side. Only then did he order them to the surface and ask for eighteen knots at a heading of almost due north. That left a few knots in reserve should they need it, but the skipper figured the additional speed would make little difference. If the submarine was spotted running on the surface, the Japanese cannon could lay down a deadly gauntlet of fire that would be impossible to outrun. The only option would be to submerge, to hide and hope they could get out of the area before shore-based patrol craft rushed to the scene to give them a migraine, or the treacherous current dragged them to shallow, dangerous water.

Charley Odom liked to joke that a clean bottom made the boat go faster. Not a clean bottom on the crew members. With no way to shower or even get a decent spit bath, that was a lost cause. No, the barnacles and other gunk that attached itself to the underside of the submarine's hull could actually slow the boat down enough that a destroyer, pursuing at a typical top speed of twenty knots, could catch a submarine that was designed to have a surface speed of twenty-one knots.

Typically, and especially in enemy-controlled waters, there were only five or six men topside when the submarine was on the surface. More could be brought up from below to man the deck gun or perform damage control if needed. But in most cases, there were three men on the bridge itself—the quartermaster of the watch, the officer of the deck, and a senior officer, often the captain. There were also lookouts in the shears—the small platform and nest of antennas and periscope supports above the bridge—men who clung tightly to their perch and, while negotiating those narrow straits, kept a nervous watch on the dark outline of shore in each direction. There were usually three lookouts. At the first flash of an artillery shot, they would scream the message, and the boat would be diving before they even heard the boom. Better to take their chances with the rushing water below than the hail of artillery on the surface.

Skippers liked to put their youngest men in the shears as lookouts, reasoning that the younger they were, the better their eyesight was. They needed to be quick, too. If the captain ordered an all-out dive and sounded the dive Klaxon twice, those men were the farthest from the hatch that led down from the bridge to the conning tower below. The second short burst of the dive Klaxon meant that the dive was already under way.

It took a *Balao*-class boat only about thirty-five seconds to go from surface running to having seawater splashing over the conning tower hatch. The boat would be sixty-five feet deep at the keel—so only the top of the periscope was above the surface—in less than a minute. By the time water reached the topmost hatch on the boat, the one from the bridge to the conning tower, everyone who had been topside had to be down the hatch and the cover closed and dogged against the sea.

The watertight hatch from the submarine's bridge led down a short ladder to a compartment called the "conning tower." This small room was where the officer of the deck (OOD) controlled the boat anytime they were submerged. It contained controls for the basic navigation of the ship, including her steering, motor speed, and the like. There was more intercom equipment here as well as the "annunciator," the device that was used to indicate speed and direction to the maneuvering room, a compartment located below the conning tower and toward the boat's stern.

There were also torpedo controls, the torpedo data computer and firing console, as well as both periscopes (one for attack and one for general observation), and the very important radar and sonar equipment. While submerged at periscope depth, about sixty feet, the submarine could effectively be controlled from the conning tower while the captain or senior officer raised and lowered the periscope to take a look around.

The officer of the deck (OOD) was the man in charge on the bridge when they were on the surface. He was the last man down the chute. Meanwhile, the diving officer assumed control of the dive itself, usually from the control room, giving the orders to the men to go to the depth and speed as ordered. Another member of the crew who was on watch in the conning tower below the bridge—usually the yeoman—had the job of reaching back up the hatch after the OOD got down the ladder, spinning the locking mechanism on the bottom side of the hatch cover, and keeping seawater from flooding the compartment. He and the OOD often got wet.

If anyone stumbled and fell on the slippery ladder coming down from the shears, was wounded, or simply did not make it to the hatch in time, there was no choice. The hatch had to be closed and locked before the water engulfed them. Any hesitation and the ship could be lost.

In nonbattle conditions, the crew might be able to stop the dive in time and the man or men left topside could be rescued. If the boat was under attack, that was not an option. Another watertight hatch led down from the conning tower downward into the control room. There was a steep vertical ladder that allowed passage between the two compartments. The "control room" is exactly what its name implies. This is the place where the boat is controlled while submerged. Various equipment typically installed here during World War II included the submergence light panel, which was popularly called the "Christmas tree" because of its display of red and green lights. Those colorful indicators let the crew see at a glance the status of various systems. Also in the control room were the bow planes and stern planes, the controls that allowed the crew to dive and surface smoothly and not too quickly. A slip here, a dive that takes too sharp a downward angle, could have sent the submarine hurtling to the bottom, out of control.

Men manning the planes, as well as the diving officer, kept an eye on the inclinometer, a device similar to a carpenter's level that told them how well they were doing in taking the boat up or down. They typically would want to remain level at a specific depth, too, and the inclinometer would allow them to do so, by "maintaining a steady bubble."

Another important device in the control room was the depth gauge. Water pressure increases one atmosphere every thirty-three feet. Descending too far could be fatal. Running too close to the surface meant the shears protruded above the wave tops, where the enemy could see them or their wake. It was crucial that submariners knew how deep they were at all times.

There was other important equipment in the control room, too, such as the ship's gyrocompasses and another type of specialized radar.

The radio room was only a few steps away. Directly below the control room, and accessed by removing deck plates, was a marvelously complicated collection of pumps, compressors, generators, piping, and blowers—the systems for keeping the boat operational and comfortable. This compartment was called the "pump room."

In the early morning hours of November 9, everyone aboard the submarine breathed easier when they emerged at the north end of Lombok Strait without incident. They could then duck beneath the cover of the Java Sea and essentially disappear.

The diving procedure on a submarine is a vital dance in which all participants must do their jobs correctly. An uncontrolled dive, because of either human error or equipment failure, can be the submarine's last. Failing to get down quickly enough in wartime, or bobbing back to the surface if some function is not performed properly or there is a mechanical problem, allows the enemy to zero in on the boat's location. That, too, can be fatal.

To begin the dive, two short blasts are sounded on the diving alarm or the officer in charge shouts, "Dive! Dive!" and the command is relayed throughout the boat. Note that three blasts on the Klaxon mean the order has been given to surface.

That simple signal sets in motion a precise series of events that the crew must perform in the proper order, and then confirm each. All engines are stopped and the boat is changed over to battery power. The doors to the engine rooms are opened even as all valves and hull ventilation are closed. Of course, the conning tower hatch is closed, too.

The bow planes—the winglike flappers on each side of the hull near the front of the submarine—are rigged for full dive so the bow of the boat will head downward, with the rest of the submarine following. The planesmen who man the stern planes must be careful to control their angle of dive. If they go too deep too fast, they could lose the ability to maintain a safe angle of attack and thus lose control of the boat.

All the while, the diving officer is barking commands, collecting reports, and keeping an eye on the status lights on the "Christmas tree." A "green board"—all lights burning green and not red—meant that all openings to the sea were in the proper position for a safe dive.

At that point, water is rushing into the tanks, the boat is growing ever heavier, and air from the compressed air tanks is bleeding into the ship's compartments for breathing. Many complicated and vital events occur at once, and the various gauges and indicators have to be monitored closely.

The goal of all submariners is to dive and surface the same number of times.

As the boat approaches its desired submergence depth, the diving officer gives the command to level off. On the surface, the crew has little concern about keeping the boat level, bow to stern. The sea does a good job of that. But as tanks are filled and emptied, as men move about the compartments, as the heavy torpedoes are fired, as diesel fuel is burned up, even as groceries are used up, the balance of the boat shifts—sometimes slowly over time, sometimes in seconds. Those on duty in the control room must be constantly vigilant to keep the boat level, to "maintain trim" or "keep an even bubble," a reference to the inclinometer.

When the submarine reaches the ordered depth, the diving officer reports to the conning officer that condition, and also the crucial fact that "trim" is satisfactory.

Once through Lombok Strait, *Billfish* promptly dived and went to two hundred feet. They aimed their bow directly north, toward the next needle to be threaded, the mouth of the Makassar Strait.

Almost two years before, in January and February 1942, Makassar had been the site of the first American surface naval action of World War II. In an attempt to thwart the Japanese invasion of the East Indies, a group of Allied destroyers engaged the enemy in a series of brutal skirmishes in and around the strait. Historians later dubbed the action the Battle of Makassar Strait.

Enemy airpower—thirty-seven highly effective dive-bombers, to be exact—proved to be the difference in that battle. Despite the Allied ships' success in slowing down their march, the Japanese did eventually control the area, including this vital passage through which *Billfish* hoped to safely transit.

Makassar Strait is 450 miles long and ranges from about 70 to 250 miles wide. Like Lombok Strait to the south, the exchange currents are treacherous and, for that reason, submarines also preferred making this run on the surface if possible. Regardless of that preference, the skippers were always one "Dive! Dive!" away from plunging to the depths if the sudden appearance of the enemy made it necessary.

Lucas and *Billfish* did some of both as they approached the southern end of the passageway to the Celebes Sea.

Early on the tenth, making fourteen knots on the surface of the

Java Sea, a target popped up on the SD radar eight miles away. Lucas, still running this modern boat the same way the Navy taught him to run the old S-boats, felt his primary goal was to get through the strait undetected and without incident, and continue on to the South China Sea. That meant not engaging the enemy unless he was practically on a collision course with them.

"Rig for dive," he commanded without hesitation. The officer at his arm there on the bridge frowned a bit but went about relaying the order. The captain knew what he was doing. And even if he did not, he *was* the captain.

"Ship rigged for dive," came the response shortly after from below.

"Clear the bridge!"

Lucas was obvious in his intentions as well as his commands. He ordered them down to two hundred feet—well past periscope depth at sixty-five feet—obviously without even considering investigating any further the rather interesting blip that had popped up in the middle of their radar screen.

Two hours later, he brought them up just far enough for the radar antenna to break the surface and to have a quick, safe look through the periscope. Nothing was visible by either means, so he gave the command to take them on up. The bow of the boat pointed upward until they were once again floating on the surface, her decks drying quickly.

"Low-pressure blower secured," the diving officer reported, then continued the litany. "All main ballast tanks dry. Safety and negative flooded. Conning tower hatch and main induction open."

Lucas ordered the charge on the batteries topped off and that they assume a speed of fourteen knots, maintaining a course just east of north.

Later that afternoon, lookouts could see in the far distance what appeared to them to be native fishing vessels. Captain Lucas quickly steered them away from any possible contact, though they seemed to be harmless enough.

"In light of later events, there may be some 'spotters' in this group," he wrote in the deck log. It was wise to be wary. The Japanese often used innocent-looking fishing craft as picket boats. They were equipped with communication and navigation equipment and immediately reported any American activity that came within their view.

By avoiding any contact with other vessels, *Billfish* was making good progress. Despite how well patrolled this strategic passage was, they had encountered nothing they could pinpoint as an enemy craft. So far, nothing that could be classified as a true, attackable target, either. Though Lucas had pointedly avoided a couple of possible encounters, there was no real reason to question his judgment in either instance.

For those men who were topside, it was a pleasant enough evening. The lookouts could catch the occasional aroma of flowers and soil, borne by the trade winds across the stretch of water from Borneo. Seagulls played in their wake, feasting on anything the submarine's screws churned to the surface.

Now the radar sweeps returned no echoes other than the tiny islands north of Bali. Radio traffic was nil except for an occasional coded message that held little interest to those aboard *Billfish*. There was no sign of *Bowfin* since they last saw her near Exmouth. It appeared she was not making nearly the excellent progress that Lucas and his boat were. If there was a race to the patrol area, *Billfish* was going to win it.

On the bridge, Charlie Rush was serving as officer of the deck. He gazed all around through his binoculars, always alert, but enjoying the warm early morning sun on his back. He still had not formed an opinion of his new skipper. That was deliberate. Rush knew he'd learned from both of his former commanders, the bad one and the excellent one. But he also had learned not to make snap judgments, and especially about a skipper who clearly had the confidence of the squadron brass.

Frederic Lucas seemed competent enough. His orders to the crew were crisp and precise. He appeared to know what he was doing at the helm of a submarine, even if it was quite a different model from the only other one he had commanded.

Still, Rush overheard scuttlebutt from those who were on their second patrol with Lucas. Reports that he preferred running and hiding to boldly confronting the enemy. That he had passed up several attack opportunities rather than risk the boat even in the slightest. That his "joint operation" with *Bowfin* was all *Bowfin* and no *Billfish*.

Rush decided to withhold judgment. The stuff he overheard could just as easily be the typical grousing of sailors working in tight, smelly quarters under stressful conditions.

But he knew one thing. Frederic Lucas was not "Moke" Millican. Each skipper had his own style, his own personality. Lucas certainly had a history in submarines, albeit when nobody was shooting at him or dropping depth charges on the boat he commanded. Or submarine experience obtained from behind a desk at staff headquarters.

Millican, though, would have found out what that return on the radar was, and if it flew the Rising Sun, he would have gone in shooting. Maybe he would have stayed away from the fishing boats, as Lucas had. Maybe not.

Now, as they made their way across the Java Sea, Rush leaned casually against the rail and listened to the lookouts in the shears above him picking at each other, exchanging opinions about the looks of each other's girlfriend back in Fremantle, arguing about the chances of their favorite baseball teams reaching the World Series next season.

"Stay alert, boys," Rush told them during a lull. He knew they were doing just that. He called them "boys" though he was only a few years older. "It can't be this easy all the way to the South China Sea."

"Aye, sir," they both answered. Several minutes passed before they resumed their good-natured arguing.

Charlie Rush grinned, cranked a bit more lens into his binoculars, and made another sweep of the horizon. If he had not known what lay ahead of them, he would have considered it a nice, casual voyage.

But he knew. He had been in these waters many times before.

11 November 1943: Proceeding through Macassar [sic] Strait, north of Cape William, on the surface at 14 knots.

0920. Sighted ship bearing 051 [degrees] T, about 8 miles, which appeared to be a destroyer or smaller anti-submarine vessel, angle on the bow zero. (Contact No. 1) Position: 0-22S; 118-42E. Submerged immediately.

Billfish had entered the strait and the crew carefully marked their progress. A nervous, hushed vigilance replaced the calm peace of the past few hours. They were near the equator, still steaming on the surface, heading northeast toward the narrowest bottleneck in the strait. Frederic Lucas was already planning on diving—at least to periscope depth—to make the run past that point, especially since there would still be daylight when they reached it.

That was when the lookouts suddenly spotted something suspicious off to their right, a dot on the horizon. It was still too far away to determine exactly what it was. About the same time, an ominous pip showed up on the radar screen at the same bearing.

No reason to assume it was anything else but an enemy destroyer. Not in these waters. Even though it would slow their progress through the narrow passage, it was the prudent move to dive the boat immediately.

That was exactly what they did.

Through the periscope, Lucas watched the mystery vessel head quickly to the point where *Billfish* had just pulled the plug. There was no mistaking now what kind of vessel they had dodged. It was a torpedo boat—225 feet long, a three-stacker (three smokestacks). She was easily within range of *Billfish*'s torpedoes. If Captain Lucas should decide to launch an attack against her, it would be a relatively easy assault with a decent chance of success.

Miss her, though, and they could bring a rain of ordnance down on their own heads. And even if they were successful in sinking her, Lucas reasoned, they would call down a bunch of other enemy vessels and warplanes right on top of them, and especially at that point in the strait that could be a really bad thing.

"Decided against torpedo attack due to small size and glassy sea which made periscope observations hazardous," Lucas wrote.

Reasonable assumption about the periscope. Though small and inconspicuous, the scope of a submerged moving vessel left a streak of foam on a calm sea. Lookouts on antisubmarine warships were trained to spot just such a marker.

Lucas backed his scope down into its sheath before the patrol boat got closer. He ordered the crew to go deeper and maintain a course that took them away from their diving point, leaving the enemy warship behind. As best he could determine, the warship had not seen them, nor did she have any reason to suspect they were there.

Drive away. Remain undetected. Make it to the patrol area in one piece and with a full complement of torpedoes. Do far more damage up there near Indochina without poking at the hornet's nest way down there in the narrow Makassar Strait.

1407. Sighted smoke bearing 071 [degrees] T (Contact No. 2). Commenced approach and target was made out to be another torpedo boat, probably Otori *or* Chidori *class, making high speed.*

Now that they were running submerged, making only eight knots or so, Charlie Rush was on duty in the conning tower as diving officer. They stayed at about two hundred feet beneath the surface for the most part, operating comfortably, and reasonably safe from detection at that depth. It was only when the vessel went down about twice as far—to better than four hundred feet—that the pressure of the seawater began to do nasty things to the hull and the ship's plumbing, not to mention the nerves of her crew. Captains of submarines ordered such dives only in the direst of circumstances.

Every ten minutes or so, doing as ordered and following standard procedure, Rush took the boat up to about sixty-five feet. That was shallow enough that he could poke the periscope just above the wave tops in the strait and have a look around.

It was on one of those bobs to the top—the tenth or eleventh, a few minutes after two o'clock in the afternoon—that he saw something that caused him to catch his breath.

Smoke on the horizon, back toward the east, in the direction of the island of Celebes. Smoke meant a ship of some kind. Was it a potential target or was it something they would be best to once again remain clear of?

Captain Lucas was not in the conning tower. He had gone down to the officers' wardroom to get a bite of supper. Rush steered in the direction of the smoke. It took him only ten seconds to see what kind of menace it was beneath that black cloud. Then, moments later, he saw enough to deduce where the enemy vessel was headed and to make a good guess about what its intentions were.

He put the scope down and sent word for the captain to interrupt his meal and come to the conning tower.

"What do you have, Mr. Rush?" Lucas asked when his head popped through the hatch from below. He still chewed the last bite he had taken, and he held a cloth napkin with which he casually wiped his lips as he listened to his young officer's report.

"Smoke on the horizon, about 070 degrees. I thought we should take a look. She appears to be a gunboat, and she's coming our way fast. I think she knows we are here and she's coming over to have a look."

Lucas gave him an odd look. Then he folded his napkin and gently draped it across a nearby pipe.

"Let me take a gander."

The skipper embraced the periscope barrel and slowly moved it back and forth in a short arc, surveying the sea in the general direction in which Rush had been looking. Then he stopped and stared hard at something for half a minute.

"I see it now," he finally said. "Another torpedo boat. You are correct, Mr. Rush. *Otori*-class. Maybe *Chidori*. She's making high speed, all right, but I do not agree that she is coming this way. I don't think she has us at all."

Either type of warship bristled with weapons, including torpedoes that could be shot through tubes similar to what *Billfish* carried, deck guns, and plenty of depth charges. They could also make better than thirty knots and drew only a few feet of water. They were extremely hard to hit with a torpedo. Or to drive away from, even on the surface. The *Otori*- and *Chidori*-class gunboats were small but very fast and maneuverable vessels. Because of their limited range, they were primarily used for coastal patrols and for enforcing blockades.

They were small but deadly.

Lucas continued to gaze almost casually through the scope. He hummed a soft tune as he moved the barrel slowly around so its optics pointed toward the front of the submarine. Charlie Rush glanced at the calibration on the scope barrel.

About ninety degrees from starboard. The enemy vessel was now almost dead ahead of them. Rush knew the son of a bitch would be clipping their periscope shortly if they did not do something.

At the speed the warship was making, and combined with the forward speed of *Billfish*—slow as the submarine might be while submerged—they would both reach the same part of the Makassar Strait in short order.

"Yes. I see what he is doing now," Lucas said, pursing his lips. "He's zigzagging. The angle on the bow is now . . . what? . . . ten degrees. He is not sure what is out here, so he is zigzagging to avoid attack."

Rush's stomach fell. Either his captain was in denial of the obvious or he was an absolute idiot! No patrol boat or destroyer was going to zigzag to avoid contact. If they were varying course, it was to try to find the exact location of the American submarine so they could blow her to hell without wasting too many barrels of TNT in the process.

"Captain, he is not zigzagging," Rush said, just loud enough to be heard over the ambient noise in the conning tower. He amazed himself with the boldness of his own contradictory words. Not even officers were supposed to question their captain's judgment, and especially not in front of other crew members.

Still, Rush knew he had to give Lucas the benefit of his opinion. Doing otherwise invited disaster. "I watched him, Captain. He made right for us. He has us."

Lucas turned from the periscope, a deep frown on his face as he looked hard at his young diving officer. It would not have surprised anyone in the conning tower—including Rush—if the captain had relieved Rush as diving officer on the spot and ordered him to his quarters.

Instead, he rubbed his chin, pursed his lips, and stated his own opinion about what he saw through the scope.

"Impossible, Mr. Rush. He is much too far away. He cannot have seen us. Not our periscope. He is almost two miles away and going past us on his latest zig. He is likely headed south to intercept one of our sisters. Maybe *Bowfin*." As if to emphasize the point, Lucas looked through the scope again, now whistling the same tune he had been humming before. "Yes, he is zigzagging. No doubt about it. He has no idea we are down here. Nonetheless, we will stay at periscope depth and maintain course, bearing 045. Use the scope only if necessary until she is well past us. I will resume my dinner. Please call me if anything changes or you see anything else that bothers you, Mr. Rush."

Charlie Rush swallowed hard. If what he had said before bordered on insubordination, what he was about to say would be a giant step closer to mutiny. Still, he knew he had to say it. Keeping quiet was never an option. In his estimation, not speaking up would be tantamount to surrendering to certain death.

"With all due respect, Captain," he started, and suddenly realized that he could not go back after uttering those words. He willed his voice not to break. Rush knew what he had seen in the periscope before the skipper took over. There was no doubt about his diagnosis of the situation. He had picked up more than tips and tactics from "Moke" Millican. He had acquired a keen instinct about Japanese captains and their tendencies. He had to make this captain understand what a precarious situation it was in which they had found themselves. "He has us. He is coming on an intercept course and will be pinging us in a few seconds. He knows we are here. Maybe those fishing boats we passed had some picket boats mixed in among them. Maybe the gunboat caught a glint of sun off our optics. However it was that he came to know we are here, he knows. I'm telling you, Captain, if you don't do something right now, we are all dead."

The control room on USS *Billfish* was nearly silent. Each crew member had his head down, doing his job, but they all heard what the fourth senior officer aboard had just told their skipper. The new kid, just about a year out of the Academy and with less than two weeks in the *Billfish* wardroom. The young man who had never even been to sub school. They had just heard him boldly challenge the opinion of one of the more experienced submarine captains in the U.S. Navy.

Never mind that Rush had been on far more war patrols than Lucas had. That he had been blessed with "Moke" Millican's on-the-job training.

But just then, as if on cue, the awkward silence in the conning tower was broken by the watery *ping! ping! ping!* of close-by Japanese sonar.

Dangerously close-by sonar.

CHAPTER SEVEN

SOMEWHERE SOUTH OF HELL

"The most difficult thing is the decision to act; the rest is merely tenacity. The fears are paper tigers. You can do anything you decide to do."

—Author and adventurer Robyn Davidson

1 *450. At a range of 3600 [yards], target appeared to have got by so abandoned approach. At this point he commenced pinging and turned toward us to present a 10 degree angle on the bow, at slow speed.*

Charlie Rush was still surprised that Captain Lucas had not relieved him from his watch and had him taken into custody. Instead, the captain simply stood there, his hands still on the grips of the periscope, with an odd, puzzled look on his face.

"Well, Mr. Rush, what should I do?" he finally asked.

Rush was so shocked at the question that he almost forgot to answer it, but the pinging was growing louder, their stalker even closer.

Captains never ask junior officers on a ship what they should do. And certainly never in front of any other crew members.

"Shoot him or go deep!" Rush told him. "Shoot him or go deep, Captain."

"I can't shoot him. He's too shallow and his angle is too small. We would never hit him."

"Then I'm going deep," Rush said.

"Well, Mr. Rush, you are the diving officer . . ." Lucas began, but Rush was already giving the order to take them deeper as he dropped down the ladder from the conning tower to the control room. ". . . but do not make any noise doing so."

That statement alone indicated Lucas's inexperience. When the enemy was using echo-ranging sonar, noise was no factor. Fleeing or ducking were the only maneuvers, damn any noise it might make.

Lucas remained in the conning tower.

"I have the dive," Rush announced to the men in the control room. "Full dive on the bow planes. Five degrees down bubble. Take her down! Take her down!"

They could feel the bow of the boat ease downward slightly. The depth gauge ticked off the submersion slowly, slowly, one foot at a time. All the while, the pinging was building and they could even hear the warship's engines above the rush of air from *Billfish*'s ballast tanks and the inrush of seawater to replace it.

The Japanese warship would soon be right on top of them—less than a hundred feet above them.

"Flood negative! All ahead two-thirds!" Rush barked. "Rig for depth-charge attack. Rig for silent running when we reach four hundred feet."

The captain should have already given the command to full speed but he had failed to do so. He was probably still worried about the noise it would create. Still operating under the mistaken impression that the enemy did not yet know they were down there.

Now Rush knew he had to use the boat's propellers to drive them deeper, to go down faster than they would if he simply flooded the tanks. Yes, it would be noisy. Anybody on the surface with listening capability would easily hear them.

He called for maximum submerged power to drive them down more quickly.

However, the enemy knew they were down there already. Rush was certain of that. If the Japanese captain dropped depth charges now, with them so shallow, some of them would easily get beneath their hull. No submarine could withstand a nearby, upward-vented explosion. They would be gutted. The only way to hope to survive the inevitable attack was to get deep in a hurry.

At last they were finally nose-down and passing two hundred feet as the bow and stern planesmen fought to keep their plunging dive under some reasonable control. As the submarine went deep, the center of gravity and center of buoyancy changed rapidly. It was a constant fight to keep them from going down too fast. At the same time, juggling seawater ballast between the various trim tanks as they went down was another delicate but essential operation.

"Mr. Rush, they just went to short scale on their sonar," the sonarman reported. The pings were closer together, less than two seconds between each. The gunboat was homing in, confident it had located its victim.

Rush pursed his lips. That was dire news.

"He has us in his sights," Rush said quietly, but every man in the control room heard him. Every man knew what that meant.

Then they could all clearly hear the *clack-clack-clack-clack-clack* of the torpedo boat's screws—the distinguishing whine between the clacks further confirming it was a patrol craft—as its path slowly ambled across theirs, first just ahead of them, and then almost straight above them.

"Charges in the water," the sonarman said, his young voice amazingly calm, but they did not need his report to know. Every man in the control room heard the *ker-chug* of the depth charges for himself.

For many aboard, it was the first time. For those who had heard them before, it was no less frightening.

1500. Target showed zero angle, still pinging, so ordered 300 feet without increasing speed or using negative as it was still not believed that he had actual contact. Rigged ship for silent running and depth charge attack.

Throughout the boat, men who were on watch were at their usual positions for a dive. Those off duty were standing by to assist as needed. A few, those most recently off watch, had been trying to sleep, but now they merely lay there, doing their part to conserve oxygen but ready to jump and help if needed.

The ship's executive officer, Gordon Matheson, was up in the conning tower with the captain. Rush assumed he was giving orders to the sailors who were steering the boat, backing up his young diving officer in the control room below.

"I count six charges in the water," the sonarman suddenly announced.

The first blast came to their starboard. It was sooner than expected, awfully close, shaking the boat violently. Everyone, including those working in the control room, grabbed something solid for support. Some did not have time to brace themselves and were sent sprawling.

Emmett Carpenter, the chief of the boat (the top enlisted man aboard), was knocked down hard by the concussion. He was a boxer and remained on his hands and knees—temporarily winded from the punch—then, shaking his head, he bounced right back up off the mat, again manning his station.

The second explosion, seconds later, was even closer and a magnitude more brutal. It rocked them before everyone had regained their equilibrium from the first one. They clearly heard the *click!* of the arming device a short moment before it detonated.

Electric bulbs burst. A thick fog of dust and bits of cork insulation filtered down from overhead. Leaks spewed and hissed from behind pipes and equipment. Meters in gauges swung wildly and then settled back down, but several of their glass covers were crisscrossed with spidery cracks.

Aft, the force of the blast tore one of the main motors right off its supports, sending it askew. The concussion also split a weld loose in one of the fuel tanks that wrapped around the submarine's hull like giant saddlebags. A small but steady trickle of oily diesel fuel began bubbling up toward the surface.

Packing around a stern torpedo tube shaft blew loose with the force of the blast, allowing more seawater to force its way inside the boat.

"Depth?" Rush asked.

"Two-seven-zero."

The third blast, then two more almost simultaneously, punctuated the report. It was directly above the maneuvering room, between the after torpedo room and the engine rooms. The force of that horrendous explosion distorted the steel skin of the boat, pulling it apart at a seam, splitting a weld joint just enough that cold seawater sprayed into the compartment. It drenched the men who stood there beneath it as well as the sensitive electrical equipment, the circuit breakers inside the cubicle. It held the switches that changed the boat from diesel to electrical power and controlled the flow of electricity to the motors. Then, helped by the increasing pressure of the seawater that surrounded it, the tiny tear in their skin closed right back up again.

It was as if God turned off the spigot in answer to the men's silent prayers.

Almost immediately after, yet another powerful charge detonated not far from the stern. It forced water into one of the torpedo tubes with enough pressure that it blew out the seal around the tube door. Water flooded in, even as those on watch in the torpedo room did all they could to try to stop it. Within moments, the men were ankle-deep—then knee-deep—in surprisingly chilly seawater.

That was all six charges, as near as the sonarman could count. The Japanese captain would pause now, looking for signs that they had crushed their target beneath them. With no evidence to show it, though, they would launch another batch over them.

Back in the control room, Charlie Rush tried to concentrate on what was going on, what he should be doing to keep them afloat until they could elude the warship. He mentally calculated how long they had been down. How long it had been since the last time they were on the surface, charged the batteries, and sucked in fresh air.

This could be life-or-death math.

They'd begun their submerged run through the strait when the appearance of the destroyer or torpedo boat chased them down. That happened just after nine o'clock that morning. It was now a few minutes after three.

They had been down almost six hours already, running on battery power, using air, with no idea of how long it would be before they could safely surface. If those guys up there were persistent and *Billfish* could not find a way out from underneath them—and if the Japanese did not blow them to pieces in the meantime—it would not be long before they would have battery and air problems with which to contend, along with everything else.

Battery power would wane and they could not go, their motors starved for juice. Lights would flicker and then go out. They could use flashlights for a while, but other vital equipment that needed electricity would inevitably go down.

Air would go bad by degrees, breathed up by men working hard, then becoming mixed with acid from the batteries.

There would come a time when it would not be breathable.

Then they would have to surface or die. Still, they had a good while before things got that bad.

They could get away from these guys. Stealth was on their side. The enemy had no idea which direction they were headed or how deep they were.

So long as the bastard did not make a lucky guess with the placement of the next round of charges, they would be out of this mess soon.

1505. While trying to get through layer at 200 feet heard screws pass overhead followed shortly by a barrage of 6 heavy charges which did considerable minor damage. Went to 400 feet and commenced evasion.

Billfish was finally at four hundred feet and her crew attempted to level her off there. But she was heavy at the tail and they struggled to find trim. The ballast tanks and pumps were doing their jobs so far, despite the pounding they were taking. Then they realized what the problem was.

The flood of water through the damaged torpedo tube was dragging them down from the rear. If they did not get the flooding stopped back there, they could sink to the bottom of the strait.

"All ahead two-thirds," Charlie Rush ordered. He hoped somebody would tell him what was happening elsewhere in the boat or that the captain would communicate from the conning tower. So far, the undamaged motor was responding and they were able to continue moving forward at a good pace. They could not maintain that speed for long, though, or they would use up the batteries.

He knew the XO was up there with Lucas. But where were the

other officers? He hoped everything else was under control up and down the length of the boat.

Chief Rendernick communicated that he was running the damage control party, which was working on some problems, but they seemed to be fixable.

Then several more blasts rang out farther away from them. Farther away but they were still potent enough to shake the hull and give them a decided sideways shove.

But then a much closer one sent the submarine swaying, skewing, as if a giant hand had slapped it. The deck beneath their feet was already littered with glass, cans, coffee cups, and big, ragged blocks of cork that had been shaken loose from overhead. They kicked stuff out of the way to keep it from tripping men as they ran back and forth through the control room.

Just then, the third officer—the third in command on *Billfish* after the captain and executive officer—stumbled through the doorway into the compartment. He came from somewhere back toward the stern. Rush thought at first, from the way he was stumbling and wild-eyed, that he might be injured. Then he saw that was not the case at all.

The man's face was twisted, distorted by terror, his eyes were wide, and he was sobbing, moaning, pounding his thighs with his balled-up fists. The front of his trousers was wet where he had obviously lost control of his bladder.

"We're going to die!" he screamed pitifully, looking from face to face of the men in the room. "The next one . . . the next one is going to kill us all!"

Rush had hardly had the opportunity to get to know this particular officer yet. He had seemed a likable enough fellow, quietly competent in his job, though Rush knew little of his previous submarine experience.

Now it was clear that the man had lost control of himself. He was terrified, in full, raging panic.

The other men in the control room stared at him for a moment. Then a couple of them grabbed him and pulled him aside, out of the way of the crew members who were rushing back and forth through the compartment on the way to do a job in another part of the boat. The pharmacist's mate was already close by, in a make-shift first-aid station set up in the galley, where he bandaged contusions and put salve on a few burns. He stepped into the control room when someone called and immediately gave the officer an injection of a powerful sedative.

The pharmacist's mate knew at once what was going on with the officer. It happened. Men broke under such conditions as these. He knew there was no other option but to put the man under and get him out of the way. The experienced men aboard—including Charlie Rush—had seen submariners lose it in situations that were not nearly as bad as this one was becoming.

Who could really blame someone, considering the nature of such an attack? Nor could anyone predict until it happened who would hold up and who would break. Not until the man was actually snatched up, caught in the maw of hell.

Now the main thing was to prevent any more of the men—especially the less experienced ones—from seeing one of their leaders carrying on so. The crew could only try to minimize the damage that such an exhibition could do to others who saw it.

Still, it was a sad thing to see when an officer, someone who was chosen and trained to be a leader, the one who was supposed to inspire his men and see them through calamity, could not control his fear any better than that.

"Take him back and put him in his bunk," Rush told them. "Make sure he has sweet dreams until we get our asses out of this mess."

Most of the others aboard *Billfish* were going about their jobs, calmly and efficiently doing what they had trained to do. A few were working miracles to keep them afloat.

Back in the maneuvering room, Electrician's Mate John Rendernick, the new chief, was doing all he could do to keep electricity flowing from the batteries to the motor. If they could not move forward, it would be only a matter of time before the enemy would pinpoint their charges and do even more damage than they had done already. Rendernick was also heading the damage control effort throughout the boat, checking with men in each compartment, tallying damage, relaying it to the control room.

The maneuvering room was located above the two large electric motors in the motor room, which actually sent the submarine forward or backward, whether she was on the surface or submerged. Each of those motors drove a screw (or propeller) that was located at the boat's stern.

While the submarine was on the surface, the electric motors got their juice from the diesel engine–driven electrical generators. While the sub was submerged, their power came from the electric batteries in the forward and after battery compartments, and they had to be charged as much as possible and ready to go.

Controlling that distribution of electricity in the proper quantities fell upon crew members who were called electrician's mates. They did their work in the maneuvering room and motor room below.

Huge electrical switches were required to change over from generator to battery power or to begin charging the batteries. Those switches were located in the "control cubicle," a stainless-steel box that measured eight to ten feet on a side. The cubicle was shock-mounted to isolate the switches from the shaking and rattling of depth charges or rough seas. Two men, called "controllermen," handled the switching from the "maneuvering panel" that was located behind the cubicle.

They adjusted the rheostats and levers in response to the orders from the conning tower or control room. Theirs was an interesting dance to watch. They followed orders from the conn or bridge by maneuvering the levers, switches, and knobs in a complicated ballet, creating the correct combination to make the submarine do what the OOD or skipper wanted her to do. Because of the electricity that coursed through the cubicle and its sensitive components, this area was also susceptible to fire.

And fire and the resulting smothering smoke were something most feared by submariners. Feared even more than flood or explosion.

If the engine rooms were the heart of the submarine, the maneuvering room was its nervous system, taking instruction from the brain—the conning tower and control room—and making the vessel do what it needed to do.

After several hours of close-by explosions, and as soon as he thought he had the damage party ahead of things, Chief Rendernick went forward to the control room to inform the captain and executive officer of what they were facing at that point.

The captain was not there. The new officer, the duty officer who had first denied and then approved his promotion to chief, seemed to be running the show.

"What you got, Chief?" Rush asked him.

Rendernick braced himself against something solid as another explosion rumbled nearby.

"Sir, we're leaking pretty badly in the aft torpedo room. Through one of the tubes." He paused to catch his breath. "Chief Odom has an idea about how we might slow it down enough to get ahead of it and maybe get a handle on the flooding. It looks like one of the first explosions knocked the port main motor right off its mounts. Sheared the bolts like you had taken a hacksaw to them. We're going to see if we can jack it back in place but it will be a chore. Especially if they keep knocking us around like this. The starboard one is working okay and should get us through."

Yet another close explosion punctuated Rendernick's report.

"How about the cubicle?"

"We're still getting water in when we get a close—"

Right on cue, another charge slapped them hard, sending several men to the deck. Rendernick braced himself against the narrow doorway. One man came up wiping blood from a cut on his lip, but he kept his position as he dabbed at it with his shirttail. Surprisingly, there was still some dust and insulation that had not already been shaken loose and it peppered down on them once again.

And the *ping, ping, ping* never stopped. It wavered from louder to quieter but it never stopped.

". . . when we get a close one, but we've rigged some metal overhead so it sends the water to the bilges instead of down onto the contacts. Hopefully the pumps will hold and we can stay ahead of it."

"Everybody okay back there?"

"Lots of bumps and bruises but we're holding together, sir."

"How about the men? Are they . . . you know . . . keeping it together?"

Rendernick looked at him, and then realized what he was asking.

"Don't worry about these guys. They're holding up fine. Holding up fine. They know me or Odom will take a wrench to their skulls if they let us down."

Rush grinned for the first time in a long, long time.

"Keep us informed, Chief."

"Aye, sir."

And he was gone.

The final compartment at the far rear end of the boat was the "aft torpedo room." It was very similar to the forward room, only considerably smaller. There were only four torpedo tubes there. Whenever the boat was on patrol at sea, each of the tubes had a torpedo stored in it. Four other torpedoes were stored in the room. This gave the boat a complement of twenty-four torpedoes in the two rooms.

Of course, if one torpedo room ran out of fish, that end of the boat was effectively out of business and left the skipper with few options in an attack. There was no way to get the heavy torpedoes from one end of the submarine to the other to reload if either torpedo room ran out. Skippers had to always be cognizant of how many fish were left and where they were located.

The after torpedo room also had its own emergency escape hatch with a supply of Momsen lungs. It also had the watertight door that could be closed to keep the boat from flooding should there be a massive leak back there. A leak like the one they apparently had at the moment.

Charlie Rush had lost track of time, but by then they had already been under almost continuous attack for three or more hours. How many charges did those sons of bitches have up there? And how long would they keep tossing them overboard until they gave up on sinking *Billfish*? How in hell did they even know they were still there and had not slunk off?

The sonarman seemed to read his mind.

"Sir, I hear three sets of screws now. There are at least three of them up there."

So, they were taking turns throwing haymakers at them.

"Take us to six hundred feet," Rush finally ordered. There had been no guidance from above—at least from the captain above them in the conning tower—so Rush had decided to act on his own and ask for permission later.

Besides, it was better to have the pressure of the water crush them than have one of those depth charges get under them and finish them off with a well-placed punch below the belt.

When they got there, they would be almost two hundred feet deeper than *Billfish* or Charlie Rush or most of the men aboard had ever ventured before.

1640. After much leisurely listening and pinging during which the torpedo boat stayed right on top of us, received 6 more charges, apparently set deeper than the first, but we were then at 465 feet and they were less effective. Again heard screws through the hull before the charges. Shortly thereafter another A/S vessel joined in the hunt.

(Note: "A/S" means "antisubmarine.")

It was at about that point in the ordeal that the men first began noticing the terrible condition of the air in the control room. It was thin, and seemed to burn their lungs when they gulped in deep breaths of the stuff. None of them wanted to consider the chemical makeup of what they were now breathing. Some were already feeling dizzy and short of breath, and it seemed something had sapped the strength from their muscles.

All this time, the explosions continued, sometimes close together, sometimes ten minutes apart—some close, some farther away, all terrifying—and they could hear the sonar pinging, sometimes loudly, sometimes not so much, and the continual clatter of the enemy ships' propellers like the rattling breathing of some prehistoric predator hot on their trail, tracking them down.

Charley Odom would later write, "Nobody can describe a depth charge attack to a layman so that it could be understood. It must be experienced. The pinging overhead and the propeller noises roaring like freight trains, as they hurry away from the coming explosions, are nerve-racking."

Meanwhile, *Billfish* was literally dragging tail. The crew had to keep the bow of the boat pointed upward at a seventeen-degree angle and maintain the engines at two-thirds speed just to keep them level and buoyant at six hundred feet. If the flooding continued, they would be standing on their tail and it would be impossible to stay at the desired depth. They would either sink until the ocean floor stopped them or they would be forced to surface in the middle of those mad-hornet torpedo boats.

Charlie Rush prayed it would not be his decision to make about which one to make happen. Somehow, though, he doubted his captain was in any frame of mind to decide. Maybe the XO would step up and make the call.

Charley Odom later bragged that since the tail was dragging and they were hovering at such a pronounced upward angle—and the depth gauge that was indicating six hundred feet was in the control room roughly in the middle of the boat—he and his shipmates back in the maneuvering room and aft torpedo room were at least fifty feet deeper. That was well over one whole atmosphere of additional water pressure back there!

Chief Rendernick passed through again and stopped long enough to give Rush an update.

"We are trying to jack the motor back onto its mount, but every time we make some progress, we get another hard hit and it slides right back off again. We'll get it, though. Chief Odom is pumping grease into the damaged tube. He thinks he can get enough pressure in there that it will at least keep the water from flooding in." The chief shook his head. "Odom tightened the bolts on the tube as tight as he could get them and they started smoking, they were under such pressure. He had to loosen them some. We repacked the stern tube shaft and it's holding for now. I'm working on trying to get out some of the water we've got in there already so we won't be so tail-heavy."

Rendernick and Odom had organized an old-fashioned bucket brigade. They were bringing water out of the aft torpedo room a bucketful at a time and dumping it into the bilges forward, where it could be pumped out. If they could slow or stop the flood and carry some of the water out of the compartment, the boat could settle back from its seventeen-degree upward angle and be in a much better condition.

The men in the bucket brigade sweated—some bled from cuts and scrapes caused when the blasts rocked the boat and threw them down hard to the deck or against an unyielding bulkhead—and they coughed and sputtered, trying to draw in enough good air to remain conscious. Still, they kept hauling the water forward as best they could.

Charlie Rush wiped his eyes with the sweaty back of his hand. They burned and stung, and he could hardly see. The air was terrible. Damage control reported that a refrigeration line had been torn loose and a good bit of gas had escaped before the right valve was closed.

Leaking seawater had inevitably reached the battery compartment and was manufacturing enough chlorine gas to further taint the atmosphere.

Just the exertion of the men, working hard to keep the boat afloat, was using up the good air.

That was not all. A carbon tetrachloride container—the chemical was used as a fire extinguisher—had burst, too, with one of the close-by blasts, and it released that gas into the concoction that was now *Billfish*'s semibreathable air.

The only choice they had was to allow the bad gas to filter quickly out of the compartment in which it had escaped. That would spread it throughout the whole boat, diluting it so the men working nearby could survive. But at the same time it added another nasty ingredient to the ugly soup that everybody aboard was forced to breathe.

Time contracted. Men survived from one vicious explosion to the next. The sonarmen had stopped counting the explosions. The Japanese seemed to have an endless supply. The occasional lulls were heartening, but since they could still hear the screws and the sonar pinging, they knew the attack would not stop. They knew the depth charging stopped only so the ships could look for submarine parts on the surface and so they could listen for any sounds of life.

The enemy seemed determined to stalk them until they killed them. Or until they ran out of things to throw at them.

It was uncanny how the Japanese gunboats never lost track of their quarry. They stayed right on top of them, as if they had their scent or could somehow see them through six hundred feet of salty, murky seawater.

One hundred feet in clear water was certainly possible. Often more. But six hundred feet? How else could they know almost exactly where they were?

Charlie Rush was pondering that very point, trying to figure how the Japanese were able to track them like a wounded animal, when he felt a touch on his shoulder.

It was one of the other officers, Max "Red" Ostrander.

"Charlie, you need some relief? You want me to take the dive?"

Ostrander was class of '42 at the Naval Academy. He was even less experienced than Rush. Still, he had a good head on his shoulders and Rush knew he could handle it. Besides, Rush figured he could be of more help somewhere else on the boat rather than standing there on his heels, trying to keep his balance, watching the planesmen while they did all they could to keep *Billfish* from sinking by their ass end to the bottom of the Makassar Strait.

"Fine, take the dive. Thanks, Red."

He took a big swig of water and decided to climb up to the conning tower to see if he could help up there. He assumed that Gordon Matheson had things in hand, even if the captain had not known what in the hell to do in most cases so far. Maybe Rush could relieve someone and let him get some water or a cup of coffee.

Halfway up the ladder, a particularly brutal blast rocked the boat, almost tearing him loose. He hugged the rungs as hard as he could until the reverberations died down and his head cleared a bit. Then he climbed on up to the conning tower to see how he might be of assistance.

There was no way he could have been prepared for what he found when he got there.

CHAPTER EIGHT

"HE'S OUT OF IT."

"Damn the torpedoes! Full speed ahead!"

—David Farragut, Battle of Mobile Bay, August 5, 1864

E ven though he was in damned good shape, Charlie Rush was winded by the short climb up the narrow ladder to the conning tower. He shook his head and tried to take in a full breath of air, but the horrible stuff seemed to catch in his throat. It was as if his lungs refused to breathe it in. The air was even worse up there in the close quarters of the conning tower than it had been below in the control room.

The air was not the worst of it, though. Not by a long shot.

The conning tower is a small room—shaped like a cylinder about ten feet by twenty feet—and packed tightly with devices to control and steer the boat. It was usually fully manned while on the surface or while at periscope depth. It also held the torpedo data computer and the aft and forward torpedo firing panels. The periscopes dominated the center of the compartment, along with the sonar and radar consoles. A ladder on the forward starboard side led up to the bridge, and the hatch to the control room was on the forward port side. During normal submerged operations, four to six men worked in the conning tower. During a submerged at-tack, as many as a dozen men crowded into the tiny area. Those typically there at those times included the captain, who was at a periscope, a helmsman at the "steering wheel," and a radar and a sonar operator, each at his respective console.

The first thing Rush saw when he got to the top of the ladder was the executive officer. He did not look good at all. Matheson leaned heavily against one of the periscopes, literally allowing the training handles to support him, his head down. When he glanced up at Rush, his face was dark, his lips an odd blue tint. He seemed on the verge of collapse.

No one was at the helm, steering the boat.

"Gordy, you okay?" Rush asked him.

Matheson's face was blank, his eyes bloodshot, and he was clearly struggling to try to stay lucid, to focus on Rush and understand what he was saying.

"I've tried everything but nothing works," he told Rush in a ragged whisper, shaking his head, gasping for enough breath to form the words. Then he coughed deeply, holding on to the handles on the scope to keep from collapsing. It was hard to tell if the XO was talking about things not working on the boat or with his own body. The rancid air was obviously taking an even heavier toll on him than on the other men.

"Where's the skipper?" Rush asked him. Matheson nodded toward the back side of the conning tower.

"He's out of it," Matheson said, and the effort of those simple words seemed to take all the strength the XO had left. He closed his eyes and slumped to the deck.

Out of it? What the hell did that mean?

The captain was sitting on the deck, his back against the radar console, his legs crossed in front of him, his head down, his lips moving. He was talking to himself, alternately praying to the top of the compartment and then inspecting the palms of his trembling hands.

"We have to give up . . . no chance . . . surface . . . give ourselves up . . . burn the codebooks . . . Mr. Matheson . . . burn the codebooks . . . set the scuttle charges . . ."

Charley Odom may have said it best when he later wrote, "In combat there are many surprises. Personality traits come to the fore. One's own behavior might bring unexpected bravery or unexplained fear."

Another two depth charges detonated close by, nearly simultaneously, and the submarine heeled over sickeningly. The motion seemed even more pronounced up there in the conning tower, at the level of the boat's topside deck. Rush held on to anything he could grab until *Billfish* swung back vertical and finally righted herself. The upward angle seemed worse up there, too.

He stepped over to the dead-reckoning tracer (DRT), a device that indicated at all times the latitude and longitude of the submarine and traced the boat's movements on a chart placed on a tracer. It would tell him exactly the course the submarine had followed since they first encountered the patrol boat and dived.

He blinked hard.

Except for very slight variations, *Billfish* had been traveling in one direction—northeast—for the past twelve hours!

"Is this right?" Rush asked, his question directed at nobody in particular. The only other man in the compartment was the sonarman, and he was busy, still trying to count blasts and listen for the first hopeful sign that the gunboats above had lost their scent.

No wonder the Japanese warships had been able to stay above them all the way. There had been no attempt to divert, to try to lose them.

Rush shouted down the hatch to the control room.

"Chief Carpenter, send a helmsman up here on the double."

The sonarman on duty was a young sailor named John Denning. He heard Rush's request for the helmsman and pulled off his headphones, stood, and started to move to the wheel. He must have figured he could do more good there than at the console.

"No, sailor, put your earphones back on," Rush ordered. "We're going to need you to do more than count depth-charge explosions. We're going to get out from under those bastards."

When the helmsman topped the ladder, Rush pointed to the wheel; then he made an announcement that could have had awful ramifications under any other situation. There, in that place and at that time, no one questioned him at all.

"I have the conn," Rush said, without drama, and again he directed his words to no one in particular.

There was no indication that Lucas had heard him. He continued to cry and pray. The skipper appeared to still be in his own world, unaware he had just been relieved of command by a junior officer.

Matheson merely nodded weakly. The XO was hardly able to stay conscious, much less tell Rush he could not assume temporary command of *Billfish*.

With that short statement, Rush had done just that—taken command of the submarine, relieving the two senior officers who were both present in the conning tower, including the captain of the boat, in the process. In other circumstances, his action could well have been considered a firing-squad capital offense. But in reality, the decision had been remarkably easy for the young officer.

If he could get them away from this brutal and potentially fatal attack, he would deal with the ramifications of his actions later.

If he could not, the point was moot.

Either way, they had only a short time left. The air was taking its toll on the crew. Some, like the XO, were already succumbing. The batteries were growing weaker by the minute, almost depleted.

And, of course, they were only one well-placed depth charge away from going on eternal patrol.

Now Rush did not even have time to think about the awesome responsibility he had instinctively assumed.

First thing was to get them out from beneath those torpedo boats.

1900. Eight charges delivered by the two ships in a joint effort. After these reversed course through the disturbance and they lost contact for the first time.

Even with the unwavering course they had been following, the Japanese captains had to have some other way to know precisely where *Billfish* was swimming. That was the only way to explain how they could be so frighteningly accurate with the charges they were dropping and never seem to get too far from directly overhead.

So far, only their dangerously deep run had saved them. Fortunately, the Japanese captains had not yet figured that into the equation, or else they would have set their charges to detonate much deeper.

A while earlier, John Rendernick had reported that they appeared to have suffered damage to a fuel tank on one of the very first explosions. Rush deduced that they were most likely leaking diesel fuel to the surface. They might be leaking compressed air as well, similar to the way *Thresher* had shown the enemy where they were when they got fishhooked. The Japanese could be following that trail of oily water or bubbles like a locomotive riding a set of rails.

"Helmsman, put the wheel over, forty-five degrees to starboard. We're going to do a buttonhook."

Nobody questioned Rush's orders, even though he was taking

the submarine on a completely different course from the one ordered by the captain earlier. Everyone knew, too, that they were running at six hundred feet deep. Much deeper at all and the water pressure would begin to crush the boat like a tin can.

There would be little room for error in making such a sharp turn. Changing course could cause them to lose the delicate balance they had struck to stay close to level and in control. Though it was not as bad as before, their tail was still heavy, and that had to be figured into the equation. A miscalculation by a planesman, failure of a pump or compressor, the sudden loss of forward power, and they could slip downward to their horrible deaths.

Rush had done a quick run-through in his head. The flood in the torpedo room had lessened, thanks to the extraordinary efforts of Odom and his crew. And Rendernick's and Odom's bucket brigade and jury-rigged pumping system had made progress on moving water out of there. They were near a "level bubble" by then, or Rush might have hesitated about making the dramatic move he was about to send them through. Rendernick and the maneuvering room crew had kept the spewing seawater out of the cubicle and the remaining motor continued to answer the call reliably.

"Helmsman, come left full rudder, please. Two hundred seventy degrees."

Now they were doubling back, forming the rest of the broad buttonhook. Next, barring a direct hit from the depth charges, they would settle back to following exactly the opposite course they had been marking on the DRT scroll for the past half a day. At that point, they would be heading southeast, away from Celebes. Hopefully away from the Japanese patrol boats and their endless supply of depth charges.

Such a maneuver has a name today. It is called a Williamson

turn, developed by a naval reservist by that name as a means to swing back and follow a reverse course precisely. It was developed primarily to locate and attempt to rescue a man who had fallen overboard. There was no name for it in 1943, but *Billfish* was going to do one of them anyway.

Rush's execution of the maneuver had a different purpose than rescuing a man overboard. His intent was to follow exactly the oily streak they had been leaving, thus using it to hide the leaking fuel that still likely marked their course. The waters of the strait had been very calm the last time they saw them. Maybe the path that had marked their course was still there and would now veil it instead.

The depth charges continued to rain down, but once *Billfish* began her sweeping turn, they were farther away. Ironically, those blasts effectively deafened the enemy's echo-ranging sonar and they caught no whisper of the rather noisy course change that she was making. There was a reasonable chance the Japanese captains would never figure out that their quarry—which had been so reliably obliging so far—had finally made a radical maneuver to try to get away. Or at least not until it was too late to find them again.

Now, as they turned, the men aboard the submarine could hear the hull groaning anew with the strain of keeping the waters of the Makassar Strait outside their vessel. There was concern that some welds might have been weakened by the barrage, that they might give way under the intense water pressure, but the boat remained mostly watertight. There was some advantage in being aboard a late-model, low-mileage ship.

Meanwhile, even as they struggled for enough air to stay conscious, the crew members of *Billfish* were doing superhuman things to keep them afloat and alive. Rendernick and Odom had, from the very beginning of the ordeal, taken it upon themselves to get damage control parties formed and in operation, and with little or no guidance from anyone else. They tried to assign a motor machinist's mate and an electrician's mate to each station, since they were best equipped to handle mechanical problems and system leaks.

The makeshift bucket brigade continued to move water from the rear of the boat to the front, where pumps took it away. That helped make it possible to take the boat through the steep turn to get away from the charges. Otherwise, with a heavy stern and the boat unstable, the turn would have been much riskier. Pumping grease into the leaking torpedo tube did not completely stop the flooding there, but it finally slowed it down enough so that they could stay ahead of it.

Water was leaking from other places, too, and had to be pumped outside to keep the boat afloat. Charlie Rush timed the expulsion of the water to coincide with the explosions of the depth charges, allowing their din to mask the sound of the pumps ejecting the water.

In the maneuvering room, the nasty air and heat were almost more than the men on watch there could tolerate. Their eyes were so dry they could not open them. It was cooler back in the after torpedo room because, unlike their compartment, it was not surrounded by the fuel and ballast tanks. There was less than an inch of steel between the crew members and the sea. Frightening as that thought was, it still meant the coolness of the deep water that surrounded them was natural air-conditioning for that compartment.

John Rendernick set up a system in which he kept the maneuvering watch standers rotating in and out of the torpedo room. The men there offered them cool, wet towels to place on their faces and moisten their dry, stinging eyes. When they could see again, they went back forward, into the maneuvering room, and relieved a shipmate so he could come back and get some relief.

Even with the boat yawing with the nearby explosions, Charley Odom and his enginemen jacked and pushed and shoved on the big electric motor, trying to get it back onto its mounts. They would eventually need both motors online.

Some men tried to smoke cigarettes when they had a hand free. No luck. If they could even get a match to strike and stay lit, their cigarettes kept going out, no matter how hard they sucked on them to try to keep them aglow. There simply was not enough oxygen in the air to keep the embers ignited.

They purposely ignored the meters that hung on bulkheads throughout the boat that indicated the amount of explosive hydrogen gas in the air. So far, that had not been a problem as the batteries dragged down instead of being recharged. It was the carbon monoxide, the carbon dioxide, and the chlorine, along with the lack of oxygen, that were robbing them of precious breaths.

Once he had *Billfish* steaming back down the opposite course they had just been following, Charlie Rush kept his eye on the DRT. He made sure they remained precisely on their previous track, including the very slight turns they had made. With any luck, the currents up there had still not erased the oily track they had left, and the fuel that was still leaking would not make much difference. It would be dark, too, and the marker would be more difficult for the surface ships to follow.

"Hey, they're searching away from us!" Sonarman John Denning said, the excitement clear in his voice now. Weary as he was, he might just as well have been singing a sweet, sweet song.

The pinging had faded noticeably. A few depth charges exploded, but they were far enough away that they caused no more problems.

Still, Rush kept them down and deep, easing away from the enemy warships at eight knots and still at over six hundred feet. Rush was having trouble breathing now. And he felt dizzy, disoriented.

He fought the temptation to simply lie down on the deck and go to sleep. It was so tempting to give the order that would send them up to the surface in a hurry. There they could open the hatches, crank the diesels, and let the big engines suck fresh air into the submarine. Those who were sick from the bad air could recover. They could assess what could be fixed and what could not and get to work. They would be able to begin putting a charge on the dying batteries.

He knew better. It required great discipline on his part to avoid the temptation to at least go up to periscope depth and have a look around. Especially when he looked into the faces of the men who were there in the conning tower with him.

No, he did not want to surface too soon and too close to their tormentors, not even to poke a periscope above the surface. He could not run the risk of their being spotted, of reigniting the attack now that they had found a way to get away from it. They could never outrun those fast vessels on the surface. They simply did not have the batteries or air to submerge and stay down long enough to elude them again.

Neither the men, the batteries, nor *Billfish* could tolerate much more.

CHAPTER NINE

"EVASIVE MEASURES . . . FUTILE."

"People never lie so much as after a hunt, during a war or before an election."

—Otto von Bismarck

1 *2 November 1943: 0025. Surfaced in full moon and glassy sea and cleared the area.*

The entries in *Billfish*'s deck log between 0920 on November 11 and 0025 on November 12 (and reproduced in their entirety above and in the previous three chapters as well as in the appendix of this book) comprise the complete "official" account of one of the more intense depth-charge attacks in World War II. The patrol report, submitted after the completion of the run once they got back to squadron headquarters, was only marginally more informing. That document would further contain blatantly misleading information as well as some notable exclusions.

Some crew members who were there would later put the total duration of the Japanese depth-charge assault on *Billfish* at over twenty hours. Others thought it was closer to twelve. In several interviews and in an oral history, Charlie Rush maintains it was at least sixteen hours from initial contact until their eventual surfacing.

Pardon them if they were not too interested in keeping up with the total time it took to live through that event. They were busy at the time.

The sonarmen specifically reported hearing the screws of at least three ships stalking them that Armistice Day night. A good sonarman—and *Billfish* had several—can deduce an amazing amount of information from what he hears on his headset.

No one could possibly estimate the total number of depth charges hurled at *Billfish* by the Japanese during the assault. Many were simultaneous. And after a while, it did not seem to matter, so they stopped trying.

Most warships in the class of boat that was believed to be their attackers' that night carried a complement of twenty-four depth-charge barrels. That means that if there were indeed three warships on their trail, they could have had as many as seventy-two "ash cans" among them to use that long evening to pound the American submarine. Since they had *Billfish* dead to rights, there would have been no reason for the Japanese not to use all they had on board. Also, since they controlled the islands on either side of the strait, it would have been possible for them to easily replenish their stock as the day wore on.

As we have seen, the damage to the submarine was significant.

Now, let us compare that testimony and conjecture to the "official" account of the incident.

Captain Frederic Lucas, in his report and as reproduced here, placed the first charges of the attack at 1505 and the last at 1900, a period of slightly less than four hours.

There was only one enemy warship mentioned in the log and report at the beginning of the assault, then a second warship that arrived later.

Though acknowledging that the first charges that exploded were "heavy," the captain specifically counted a total of only twenty depth-charge explosions in the deck log. He does not classify any of the others as "heavy" or particularly close by.

Lucas allows for only "considerable minor damage," and that damage occurred as a result of the first set of six "heavy charges" at 1505.

No other damage or injuries are mentioned in the official report, with two exceptions. And while there was a more complete description of the evening's events in the captain's patrol report narrative, it is quite different from the way the crew members remembered what happened.

As part of each postpatrol report, the captain of a submarine was required to make notations and write a narrative account in several specific categories, including "Weather," "Radio," "Radar," and "Density Layers." One category was called "Major Defects and Damage." Lucas listed no "Major Defects," but under "Damage," he indicated, "The only important damage from the depth charge attack on 11 November was the chipping and specking of the upper prism of number two periscope which made this periscope almost useless for the remainder of the patrol."

No mention of the damaged fuel tank that leaked to the surface. Nothing about one of the main motors being ripped from its supports. Not a word about one of the aft torpedo tubes leaking so badly that a bucket brigade had to haul water out of the compartment to a place where it could be pumped out of the submarine—damage that almost caused enough flooding that they were in danger of losing the boat.

Most observers would consider each of those, as well as other damage that occurred in the attack, far more significant than the specking of the prism in a periscope.

Then, under "Health, Food and Habitability," Lucas wrote under the subheading "Health" that "there were five admissions to the sick list with diagnosis and number of sick days as follows:

1 (officer) submersion	3 sick days
1 (officer) intercranial injury	5 sick days
3 Gonococcus infection, urethea [sic]	0 sick days"

We can only surmise that the submersion casualty was the executive officer, Gordon Matheson, and that would be an accurate description of what happened to him. Missing was any reference to the third senior officer, who was given an injection by the corpsman and put to bed in his quarters. Unless that was the officer whom Lucas referred to as suffering an "intercranial injury" that put him out of commission for five days.

And we can assume the gonococcus infection was unrelated to the brutal depth charging in the Makassar Strait on Armistice Day.

Finally, the captain's most complete account of the ordeal in the official report came under the heading "Anti-Submarine Measures and Evasion Tactics." There, in its entirety, he reported:

"The Otori or Chidori torpedo boat encountered on 11 November in Macassar [sic] Strait was remarkably effective both in original detection and in staying right on top of us for four hours.

"Apparently he was aware of our presence in the vicinity, probably having been informed by aircraft, 'spotters' on small sailing vessels, or by the first torpedo boat which we thought we had evaded without being detected. It is believed that he sighted our periscope at a range of approximately 3600 yards even though it was being used with extreme care because of the calm sea.

"All attacks were very deliberate, unhurried, and well executed. He did not waste a charge. He sat for long periods almost directly over us, so that his auxiliaries could be plainly heard on the JP sound equipment, alternantly [sic] listening and pinging, just kicking ahead occasionally to stay with us. All evasive maneuvers at silent speed were futile.

"When entirely satisfied of our position he would start in for a run, but several times he apparently lost echo-ranging contact earlier than he expected because of our deep submergence (465-480 feet) and would stop and start the procedure all over again. This was especially aggravating as we had by this time become very heavy, requiring a 16 [degree] up angle to maintain depth, and were waiting for the next charges so that we could blow water from safety.

"On each of the three dropping runs his screws were plainly heard through the hull 15-20 seconds before the charges.

"The effectiveness of the attack seemed to be reduced rather than enhanced by the arrival of the second A/S vessel and contact was finally broken by doubling back through the disturbance caused by 8 charges dropped in a coordinated attack."

No indication of why the ship was "very heavy" or of any damage that might have caused it. No notation of Rush, Rendernick, or Odom and the amazing lengths to which they went in order to save the ship. No confirmation of going over two hundred feet below test depth. Wrong details about how they eventually escaped the attack alive. A claim that "evasive measures at silent speed were futile" when there were apparently only minimal attempts to evade anything until Rush assumed command in the conning tower and made the first turn in half a day.

No mention of anyone being "out of it."

Charlie Rush flatly maintains that the *Billfish* captain "falsified the patrol report" so that none of what happened would get out.

Of course, when they finally returned to home port, there was no attempt to honor those men who performed so bravely in the face of death. That would have to wait.

Have to wait for sixty years.

As *Billfish* made her way on toward her patrol box in the South

China Sea as if nothing profound had happened, limping along on one motor for a while, the crew repairing what they could, Rush had a difficult decision weighing on his mind.

If Frederic Lucas did not write him up on charges—and Rush saw no indication that his captain would ever speak a word to anyone about the impromptu assumption of command—and since they had escaped the attack alive, should the young lieutenant simply forget what had happened? Or did he owe it to future submarine crews, to the war effort, and to Lucas himself to make somebody at the squadron level aware of what happened?

Make them aware and let the chips fall where they may.

Trouble was, he doubted anyone back in Fremantle would believe him or the crew if Captain Lucas maintained otherwise.

Then something happened that made Rush's decision unnecessary. Something that would keep the Armistice Day episode in the Makassar Strait a complete secret—beyond the hull of *Billfish*—for the next six decades.

At the same time, the extraordinary courage of the *Billfish* crew under the most intense situation imaginable would also remain unknown to anyone who was not aboard SS-286 and a part of what happened that terrible afternoon.

CHAPTER TEN

DANGEROUS GROUND

"It is better to conquer yourself than to win a thousand battles. Then the victory is yours. It cannot be taken from you, not by angels or by demons, heaven or hell."

—Buddha

They could no longer hear the screws of the Japanese ships no matter how hard they listened. Almost an hour had passed since the last depth-charge explosion and it was blessedly quiet up there.

Billfish eased farther away still, coaxing the last few amperes of current from the overheated battery cells, putting as much distance between them and their tormentors as they dared before risking coming to periscope depth and taking a look.

There was always the chance they would meet other warships coming their way, but Charlie Rush knew they needed to surface as soon as practicable and take their chances. The air they were breathing in the boat was the biggest problem. It was rife with deadly carbon monoxide, carbon dioxide, and irritating chlorine fumes. If they could get some of the bad air vented out and get some charge on the batteries, they might be able to dive again in a hurry and stay down another couple of hours should they encounter yet another enemy warship.

"Come to periscope depth," Rush finally ordered.

He stopped the boat, too, afraid what little wake the scope might produce on the calm sea could be spotted by the frustrated enemy lookouts.

He was already walking the periscope around in a circle when its top poked above the sea's surface. The temptation was to look back toward the stern first, back to where he knew the destroyers were. However, he was obligated to take a good look all the way around anyway, just to make certain nobody had slipped up on them, and they were no longer hearing the sounds of their tormentors.

At last, he looked back in the direction from which they had just escaped. In the far distance, he could just make out the lights of three ships, their running lights blazing, searchlights brilliantly illuminating the surface around them. Clearly, they were attempting to relocate their prey, to catch sight of the telltale leak. Or maybe still trying to spot debris floating to the surface from a destroyed American submarine. The Japanese patrol boats seemed to be not one bit concerned that the submarine they had been bombarding for better than half a day might offer any threat to them.

Rush remained at the scope for several more minutes, alternately checking the known attackers in the distance and looking for others, unknown and approaching from other headings. He did not see anybody.

"Stand by to surface. Rig for surface."

When the curvature of the earth finally hid the Japanese ships from view, Rush brought *Billfish* to the surface with three quick blasts on the Klaxon.

"Low-pressure blower secured," the diving officer reported. For all practical purposes, Charlie Rush was now the captain of *Billfish*. "All main ballast tanks dry. Safety and negative flooded. Conning tower hatch open. Depth eighteen feet."

USS *Billfish* (SS-286) during sea trials, probably on the Thames River near Groton, Connecticut, in 1942. She went to war in the summer of 1943.

U.S. Navy

Lieutenant Commander (later Commander and Captain) Frederic Lucas, skipper of USS *Billfish* for her first two World War II patrols.   *U.S. Navy*

The *Billfish* at pier, probably in Pearl Harbor, Hawaii, in 1943.
U.S. Navy

USS *Bowfin* (SS-287) in Fremantle, Australia, in 1944.
U.S. Navy

Admiral Ralph Waldo Christie (*right*), in one of his trade-mark dockside ceremonies, presents the Presidential Unit Citation to Commander Joseph Willingham and the crew of the *Bowfin* upon her return to Fremantle from her first war patrol.   *U.S. Navy*

Commander Willingham (*center*) reads his orders during the commissioning ceremony for the *Bowfin*, May 1, 1943.   *U.S. Navy*

Admiral Ralph Waldo Christie, commander of the submarine squadron at Fremantle during a portion of the period covered in this story. Christie was a flashpoint for controversy throughout the war. *U.S. Navy*

Admiral Charles Lockwood, the commander of the submarine squadron at Fremantle, Australia, when *Billfish* and *Bowfin* became the first two boats to operate from there. He later became commander of submarines in the Pacific. *U.S. Navy*

"Moke" Millican's *Thresher* passing beneath a bridge on the Thames River, New London, Connecticut, possibly during her sea trials, getting ready for war. Charlie Rush, one of the *Billfish* heroes, served as an officer under Millican on *Thresher* and was often his gunnery officer.
U.S. Navy

USS *Escolar* (SS-294), at her launch at Cramp Shipyards in Philadelphia. This was Millican's next command after the heroics at the helm of USS *Thresher*. She was lost with all hands in November 1944 on her first war patrol.
U.S. Navy

Prior to her doomed war patrol, an awards ceremony for the *Escolar* was held in Philadelphia during sea trials. Her captain, Commander William "Moke" Millican (*left*) presents an award to a crew member.
U.S. Navy

View from the bridge of a *Balao*-class submarine, running on the surface at near top speed of about twenty knots. *U.S. Navy*

An electrician's mate at work in the maneuvering room of a WWII submarine. The switches, rheostats, and other equipment in this compartment sent power from the generators to the batteries for charging or to the electric motors directly below. *U.S. Navy*

Crew members man the controls for the planes in the control room. These "wings" on the outside hull of the submarine enabled the crews to control dives and surfacing and to maintain trim or stay level while submerged. *U.S. Navy*

A torpedo room view aboard a fleet submarine. Torpedoes weighed about a ton and a half. *U.S. Navy*

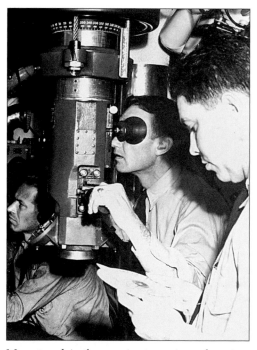

Men at work in the conning tower in a submarine. The calibration on the periscope at the top gave the direction in which the man at the scope was looking and could be entered into the torpedo data computer (TDC) to help guide the torpedoes when they were fired. *U.S. Navy*

Mary Kay Rendernick, daughter of Chief Electrician's Mate John D. Rendernick, one of the heroes of the *Billfish* depth-charge attack in 1943, inspects the plaque bearing her father's name. The Damage Control Wet Trainer at Pearl Harbor, Hawaii, was named in his honor on August 17, 2004. *U.S. Navy*

Captain (retired) Charles Rush (*right*) visits with a modern-day submariner in Pearl Harbor, Hawaii. Here he stands in front of the wet trainer that had just been named for Chief John Rendernick. *U.S. Navy*

They were finally back on the surface, and sweet tropical air spilled down the conning tower hatch when the yeoman popped it open.

Charley Odom stuck his head through the hatch from the control room below before Rush could even climb the ladder to the bridge.

"Sir, we can only get one engine to fire but we're working on the others," he reported. "We're going to have to do a slow charge on the batteries anyway. Chief Rendernick says the cells are so hot we'd make more hydrogen than we would electricity down there right now."

"Thanks, Chief. Let me know your progress."

From the bridge, Rush rang up the men on watch in the forward torpedo room. He told them to open the hatch up there to let in some fresh air. He ordered that all the watertight doors between the torpedo room and the engine room be opened, too, but with men standing by to shut them quickly if they had to make a sudden dive.

The main induction—the vents that brought fresh air to the diesel engines—was kept closed, though. With only one engine running, they could get by for a bit, and that forced more air down the hatch in the torpedo room and the conning tower, through the open doors between compartments, and across the sizzling batteries. Not only would that cool the cells, but it would also flush out the hydrogen they were now making, even as it drew out all the other bad stuff that made up the air inside the submarine.

While Charley Odom's gang worked miracles to get the other three diesel engines going, John Rendernick was busy in the cubicle, repairing the damage done by the depth-charge blasts. He also oversaw the battery-charging effort. Tired and sick as he and the rest of the crew were from their ordeal, they did not take time to rest or recuperate. Not yet. They were still treading water on the surface in very dangerous waters.

Charlie Rush had a fleeting thought. What if he had not had a change of heart and promoted Rendernick to chief at the last minute? And what if he had not made sure the man's first assignment as chief was in the maneuvering room aboard *Billfish*?

Rhetorical questions, of course. Any other submariners in Rendernick's position would likely have done the same thing and just as well, Rush thought. But who knew? Who knew?

All he knew for certain was that John Rendernick, Charley Odom, and the others became true heroes that long, horrible night.

One other thing came to mind. When they returned to Fremantle, he would make sure the brass learned about their efforts. Then they would receive proper recognition for what they had done. If Captain Lucas did not follow through on arranging for them to receive appropriate awards, Rush vowed to himself, he would somehow make certain that it happened. They deserved that much, at least.

It is unclear when Captain Lucas ultimately left the conning tower that night. In the confusion, the crush of trying to escape the hell they were in, no one noticed. Later in the day, there was little mention among the officers of what had happened or how it came to be that Charlie Rush took command of *Billfish* and, in effect, saved them and the ship.

The enlisted men were a bit more accomplished at passing scuttlebutt. Though they spoke in whispers, recounting bits of what they had heard had gone on in the conning tower, the word was soon passed from bow to stern.

They whispered because they knew better than to let an officer overhear any disparaging remarks about the captain or anyone else from the wardroom. Still, when any of them saw Charlie Rush, they poked one another, nodded, and looked at the young Southerner with newfound respect.

Otherwise, they had orders to get to a certain point in the war zone, and they did what they had to do in order to make that happen. If they repaired the damage, there was no thought of cutting the patrol short and going home. Once they got the engines working and much of the damage repaired or bypassed, they continued their journey north and northwest toward Indochina. Oddly, it appeared everything was business as usual aboard USS *Billfish* despite the most unusual events of November 11, 1943.

XO Matheson was still quite ill. He mostly remained in his bunk for the next few days, treated by the corpsman. When Matheson finally did return to full-time duty, his face still ashen and with a pronounced wheeze when he breathed, he confessed he hardly remembered much of what went on in the conning tower during the assault. No one volunteered to give him the full account and he did not ask for elaboration.

They were out from beneath those destroyers. They had survived their gut-wrenching run somewhere south of hell. Now they had to concentrate on getting to where they were supposed to be, to rendezvous with *Bowfin* and start doing some damage, all without getting themselves sunk.

12 November 1943: 1834. Surfaced 20 miles southeast of Tg. Mangalihat. Received dispatch from CTF 71 warning of anti-submarine activity in this vicinity. Set course for Sibutu Passage.

This remained a very dangerous place to be. The peninsula that jutted out from the island of Borneo at the northern end of the Makassar Strait was an important landmark. Once past, they were in the Celebes Sea, but that area, too, was swarming with enemy vessels, the sky busy with patrol planes.

"No shit!" was the reaction to the message from headquarters, to the revelation that they could expect "antisubmarine activity" in those waters.

The Sibutu Passage was yet another bottleneck, allowing them to move from the Celebes Sea into the Sulu Sea, but at great peril.

14 November 1943: 1825. Surfaced and passed through Sibutu Passage and between Pearl Bank and Doc Can Island. Full moon but nothing sighted.

A moonlit passage through a narrow stretch of water—dark slivers of land visible in the distance on each side—was a nerve-racking swim, but it was still the best way to get through. There was certainly no time to wait for a new moon or a cloudy night. Not in the Celebes, where even a simple fishing boat could be a lookout, reporting their presence to the quick torpedo boats, which could race to where they were well before they had cleared the area.

Lookouts in the shears above the bridge were extra alert. Radar scanned the surface as far as it could toss a signal and looked to detect enemy radar. Sonarmen kept their headsets pinched tightly to their ears, listening.

Fortunately, the coast of Borneo to their south and west was very sparsely inhabited. Lucas kept the submarine far enough away that they could quickly find deeper water if they had to pull the plug. Their next channel—the Balabac Strait—took them into the vast South China Sea, bordered on the east by the Philippines, on the west by Indochina and Malaysia, and on the south by Borneo, the Celebes, and Sumatra—the Greater Sunda Islands.

In company with *Bowfin* and running as an informal, two-boat wolf pack, *Billfish* would, within three days, be crisscrossing prime hunting waters. Ships from Malaysia and Sumatra, laden with rubber, bauxite, oil, and other necessities for the war effort, would be steaming north, toward the Japanese Home Islands. Running in convoys and with limited escorts, the ships would involuntarily offer themselves up as prime targets. Two submarines operating in tandem could wreak havoc until their allotment of torpedoes was gone and their supply of diesel fuel ran low.

Though not as glamorous perhaps as sinking aircraft carriers and battleships, interrupting that supply of raw materials was just as important in bringing the war to a quicker end. No war machine could operate with its supply arteries severed.

Now that they were nearing their patrol area, the mood of the crew brightened noticeably. Gossip about the depth-charge attack and what had happened in the conning tower during the depth charging gradually diminished. Men concentrated on repairing everything that had broken or busted during the ordeal. They scanned the horizon. They did what they had to do to stay in motion and prepare for the next challenge.

Finally, they would be able to do more than duck and hide and hunker down. They could strike back.

15 November 1943: Proceeding across Sulu Sea toward Balabac Strait at 14 knots.

2008. Passed through Nasubata Channel, Balabac Strait at 18 knots.

It had taken the better part of a week, but *Billfish* had finally negotiated the last of the fractured jigsaw puzzle of islands, the grassy seas, the masses of deadly poisonous sea snakes tangled up like balls of writhing yarn, the keyhole straits and channels where the currents surged against their bow. She and her crew were at last in the southeastern corner of the South China Sea.

Now their route took them through a region that bore a very ominous moniker.

16 November 1943: Proceeding toward area in South China Sea, south of Dangerous Ground, on the surface at 10 knots.

All four diesel engines rumbled now, back online just in time to make good use of their powerful push. So long as they could remain on the surface, they could keep the batteries fully charged and make better time toward the spot in the middle of the South China Sea where they were to meet up with Walt Griffith and USS *Bowfin.*

Now they were negotiating waters that look benign enough on maps, but are in reality one of the world's most dangerous places. This area has been indicated on ship charts for centuries as the "Dangerous Grounds." The area is so named because of the hazardous shoals in the area, including hidden submerged rocks, sandbanks, and coral reefs, often so numerous that ships steam into dead-end cul-de-sacs, and then have to back away and attempt to find another route through. They are so abundant—and some of the hazards shift so frequently in rough seas and frequent storms— that no chart can accurately depict them.

The area bears that apt name for another reason, too. Those rough waters have long been the object of political dispute and are, to this day, a favorite place for pirates and outlaws ready to pounce on shipping that dares to try to navigate there.

Billfish remained to the south, though, before making a sharp northward turn east of the Spratly Islands. The shoals and sandbars were especially dangerous for a submarine, and the waters often too shallow to offer them a decent hiding place. Besides, the targets they sought—military or commercial—were just as unlikely to operate there as they were.

17 November 1943: 0300. Entered area at 8—00N; 112—22E proceeding toward rendezvous with BOWFIN at Lat. 11—00N; Long. 112—00E.

2335. Arrived at rendezvous and failed to contact BOWFIN. Patrolled in area.

Some crew members had noticed that Captain Lucas seemed fixated on the meet-up with their sister submarine and her new skipper, Walt Griffith. Griffith had replaced Joe Willingham on *Bowfin* when she returned from their first patrol alongside *Billfish*, when Admiral Christie rewarded Willingham with his new command. Everyone noticed that since the depth-charge attack on the eleventh, Lucas and *Billfish* had made no special effort to seek out and engage potential targets. Granted, it was tough territory and their mission was to do damage in the South China Sea, not get themselves sunk while on the way there. Still, they were a hunter and a killer and should have been pursuing quarry.

The grumbling that had died down a bit after the depth-charging incident promptly started up again as they wandered around, looking for their sister, avoiding contact with any enemy vessel.

Later, they would learn that *Bowfin*, en route to the same area and following practically the same path through the same straits and grassy seas as *Billfish*, had been anything but passive and determined to remain out of trouble. She inflicted considerable damage on the enemy and still managed to be a couple of days ahead of *Billfish* in her transit to the waters off Indochina.

Indeed, Griffith and *Bowfin* took the time en route to the rendezvous point to sink four two-masted enemy schooners in two separate attacks and to blast the hell out of a couple of full-to-the-brim oil tankers in another.

Two of those schooners were sent to the bottom in a daring surface assault. As had become Griffith's way already on his first run at the helm of a submarine—and reminiscent of the tactics of other "ace" sub commanders like "Moke" Millican—*Bowfin* went into the fray against the enemy ships with her deck guns blazing, hoarding her torpedoes for use later in the run.

Then, still proceeding as ordered to the South China Sea,

Griffith and his crew took the opportunity to punch holes in the sides of two unescorted tankers that they encountered along the way. They employed some well-placed and perfectly timed torpedoes to set the ships and their precious petroleum cargo brilliantly afire. Someone aboard joked that he hoped Emperor Hirohito could see the billows of black smoke from his palace.

Of that attack, Griffith would later write in his patrol report: "Nice fireworks for Armistice Day."

Yes, that double sinking by Griffith and *Bowfin* occurred several hundred miles north but at almost the same time that *Billfish* was trying to swim out from beneath the vicious depth-charge attack in the Makassar Strait.

CHAPTER ELEVEN

SISTERS

"There has never been a mutiny in a ship of the United States Navy. The truths of this film lie not in its incidents but in the way a few men meet the crisis of their lives."

—On-screen message at the beginning of
the 1954 film *The Caine Mutiny*

U SS *Bowfin* and USS *Billfish* were truly twin sisters. Their hull numbers were SS-286 and SS-287 consecutively. *Bowfin*'s radio tactical call sign was "November Whiskey Quebec Victor." *Billfish*'s was "November Whiskey Sierra Lima." Their keels both were laid down on the same day, July 23, 1942, at the Portsmouth Naval Shipyard in Kittery, Maine. Shipyard workers welded their hulls and bolted them together in dry docks that were only a short distance away from each other.

Billfish was launched on November 12, 1942. The wife of one of the early submarine heroes, Lieutenant Commander Lewis S. Parks, did the honors, breaking a bottle of champagne across the bow of the new vessel.

(Lewis Parks was skipper of *Pompano* when an American antisubmarine aircraft mistakenly bombed and almost sank her. Later, after the war and after making the rank of admiral, Lewis Parks was in charge of the U.S. Navy Office of Information in Washington, D.C. While he was there, Hollywood producer and director Stanley Kramer approached the Navy about giving him technical advice and providing other assistance for a movie he was producing. Several key high-ranking Navy staff members were opposed to the film. They wanted to dissuade Kramer from even doing the picture and to withhold any support by the Navy, but Parks eventually gave his full approval. Many service members and ships were used in the making of the movie. The other admirals objected because the story line depicted an incompetent and mentally unstable ship's captain and the eventual mutiny by the ship's crew. There had never been a mutiny in the U.S. Navy, the admirals pointed out, and they did not want a motion picture—even a work of fiction based on a Pulitzer Prize–winning novel—to depict such an unthinkable thing. The film was *The Caine Mutiny*, which received seven Oscar nominations and was a top-grossing film in 1954. Parks did make one request of Kramer. Immediately after the opening credits, an on-screen message makes clear the incident portrayed is fictional, and adds, "There has never been a mutiny in a ship of the United States Navy. The truths of this film lie not in its incidents but in the way a few men meet the crisis of their lives.")

Billfish was named after a type of long-jawed fish that sported hard, tough scales and needle-sharp teeth. Billfish include the gar, marlins, swordfish, and needlefish.

Bowfin followed her sister's commissioning three weeks later, on December 7, the auspicious one-year anniversary date of the Pearl Harbor attack. Another Navy wife, Mrs. James Oliver Gawne, sponsored her.

Her namesake, the bowfin, is a voracious freshwater fish native to the Great Lakes, the upper Mississippi River valley, and nearby waters.

Frederic Colby Lucas was at the helm of *Billfish* when the Navy officially commissioned the submarine on April 20, 1943. Joe Willingham was commander and plank owner on *Bowfin* on May 1, when she was placed into commission, only ten days after her steel sibling's ceremony.

The two submarines made their way down the East Coast of the United States, through the Panama Canal, to Australia at about the same time. They were to be the first two boats attached to the new Squadron Sixteen at Fremantle, near Perth, on the Indian Ocean.

When the Japanese overran the Philippines in December of 1941 and January of 1942, the Navy's submarine base there evacuated to Dutch Harbor in Java. That spot proved inadequate for the purpose. Darwin, on the extreme northern Australian coast, and Exmouth, farther west, were considered as possible bases, but both were vulnerable to Japanese air attack. The Japanese had already conducted a brutal bombing assault on Darwin. Perth and its nearby harbor city of Fremantle were the final choice.

Captain John Wilkes was the first commander there, succeeded soon by Admiral Charles Lockwood, who went to work improving the facilities and working conditions for his submarine crews. One of his first actions was to lease several area hotels for the exclusive use of his men. The locals were also quite friendly and welcomed the Americans.

In January 1943, Admiral Robert English, Commander Submarines Pacific, died in a plane crash, and Lockwood was called to take over his job. Admiral Ralph Waldo Christie went to Australia to assume Lockwood's command. Though *Billfish* and *Bowfin* were the first boats there, by the end of 1943, thirty submarines operated out of Fremantle. However, in 1944, when the Philippines fell back into American hands, the squadron soon returned there for reasons obvious to anyone looking at a map of the region.

Ralph Christie was a flashpoint for controversy during the war. Many considered him an "old-line" submariner, a commander who clung to the belief that the boats were best suited for defensive missions and should be "risk aversive." He was also incredulous about claims by sub skippers that the Mark XIV torpedo was not performing properly.

In late 1942, the Navy sent Christie from his squadron command in Brisbane, Australia, back east, to the torpedo test facility in Newport, Rhode Island, as inspector of ordnance in charge. With his educational background, he was the perfect choice to speed along the testing process of existing weapons and to help develop the next generation of electric torpedoes. Then, when Admiral English died in the plane crash, and despite the fact that Christie had lobbied for the job that went instead to Charles Lockwood, the Pacific commander sent Christie to Fremantle instead—to replace Lockwood there.

The torpedo controversy raged on, though, and it dogged Christie even as he left Newport and traveled halfway around the planet to his new job in Western Australia. Lockwood, finally convinced there was a problem, just as his skippers had been insisting, ordered captains to deactivate the malfunctioning magnetic detectors on their torpedoes. They would rely instead on the force of the blow to set off the explosion.

Christie, who had helped develop the magnetic device in the first place, ignored those directives and stubbornly ordered Perth-Fremantle boats to continue using them. *Billfish* and *Bowfin* were still under that order when they went on their first two war patrols together. It would be January 1944 before Christie allowed his skippers to use anything else but the problematic detonator.

Even when he tried to do something special and meaningful for his men, Christie seemed to push all the wrong buttons back at fleet command. He was in the habit of meeting at pierside the beat-up boats that were returning from war patrols. The first thing they saw was the big boss in his dress uniform, surrounded by his aides. There he held an awards ceremony on the spot and gave decorations and citations to the crews.

This, of course, went against all official procedures and channels. Many, like Lockwood, felt it was a real security risk to do what he was doing. Christie was performing very public awards ceremonies, reading aloud detailed citations, and it all came quite soon after the events they honored. It was easy for the wrong people to gather information about submarine operations and movement about the Pacific. Christie's insistence on continuing this policy, even after the naval commander for the Pacific directly ordered him to stop, was eventually a major factor in his removal from the Perth-Fremantle command.

But that change did not come before the admiral did one of the most audacious things ever perpetrated by someone of such a high rank. Christie had long lobbied with his superiors to allow him to go along on a patrol with one of the skippers under his command. He felt it would be a tremendous morale booster for his crews to see that their commander was willing to put himself in their shoes—and face the same dangers as they.

His bosses always turned him down without even considering such a thing. A squadron commander was far too important a cog in the Navy's war machine to risk losing him out there where almost a quarter of the crews were dying.

Then, in January 1944, *Bowfin* and Walt Griffith interrupted a very fruitful patrol to pull into Darwin for provisions, fuel, and more torpedoes. Christie saw his chance.

Without even asking again for permission—and risking another denial—he flew from Perth to Darwin and joined *Bowfin*. He watched from the bridge as Griffith sank a merchant ship in less than a minute during a well-orchestrated surface attack. It was a sinking, by the way, for which she would never be credited, even if a squadron commander who held the rank of admiral had witnessed the whole thing. He also served as officer of the deck, manning the bridge while the crew rested up for what intelligence promised was a particularly promising convoy that was headed their way that evening.

The ensuing attack was the only time Christie questioned the tactics of his skipper during the short run. Griffith made a daring surface assault on a Japanese seaplane tender. "We were very close to him . . . too close, within machine gun range," he later wrote in his diary. "I was most uncomfortable." Griffith turned his stern to the enemy warship and fired two torpedoes at less than a thousand yards' range.

The force of the explosion was so strong and *Bowfin* was so close that when they hit, it knocked the admiral's cap off his head and into the sea and threw him against the railing so hard it broke his binoculars. The tender did not sink but was damaged so badly it was of no use to the enemy for the rest of the year.

Griffith took Christie back to Exmouth to drop him off so he could catch a plane, but not before he sank two sampans loaded with cement along the way. He had to use deck guns for that because he was fresh out of torpedoes.

The entire portion of the patrol with Christie aboard lasted only nine days. However, by taking the ride, the admiral became the first force commander and the first of his rank in history to make a submarine war patrol. He accomplished his goal of raising morale. The rank and file and the officers alike were impressed with their commander's willingness to strap on a submarine and go to where the war was very, very hot. And we have no record of any formal reprimand from his superiors for his impromptu cruise—without permission.

So the two sister submarines—the "286" and the "287"—reached Australia at about the same time and prepared to begin operations from there.

Billfish and Lucas left Fremantle for their first war patrol twelve days ahead of *Bowfin* and Willingham, but they soon hooked up to work together in a loose copatrol. As we have previously noted, *Bowfin* got the better of that effort, based on tonnage of damaged and sunk vessels.

Willingham's executive officer, William Thompson, would later write about one particularly impressive attack, "[He] was a perfectionist. We sank three ships, firing bow and stern tubes simultaneously—bow with the TDC [torpedo data computer] but stern with his infallible eye and judgment. To the best of my knowledge this was an 'only feat' during the war."

Although postwar research would not give Willingham and his boat credit for three of the ships they were certain that they sank in that assault, it was still a daring and unorthodox attack, one that quickly entered into the lore of the wartime submarine skippers. Willingham's crew knew what they and their skipper had done and they helped spread the legend around the leased resort hotels when they returned to Perth.

Willingham's boss, Admiral Christie, was equally impressed. He said the skipper's efforts were "brilliant" and promptly rewarded him with a medal presentation ceremony on the pier at Fremantle and by promoting him off *Bowfin*. He sent him off to command a submarine division in Brisbane. It was typical for a captain to recommend his replacement when he left a boat under good graces, and Willingham strongly suggested that his XO, Bill Thompson, get the job.

However, Christie had someone else in mind. He chose Walter Thomas Griffith, who had been executive officer on another submarine and had a year's worth of seniority on Thompson.

There were no hard feelings. Thompson remained second in command to Griffith and continued to learn. Based on his accomplishments when he did ultimately get his own boat, it was obvious that both skippers—Willingham and Griffith—had trained Thompson well. He later commanded USS *Cabrilla* (SS-288) and led that vessel on four successful war patrols, leaving him among the top sixty wartime submarine skippers in total credited enemy shipping destroyed.

In his writings, Christie hardly sounded as if he had a great deal of confidence in the man he made *Bowfin*'s new skipper. He described Walt Griffith as "studious looking, red-haired, a trim young man with blood pressure too high and a slight hand quiver."

XO Bill Thompson was more flattering in his take on his new skipper. He wrote, "[He] was absolutely fearless—maybe too much so—and a reasonable and wonderful skipper and shipmate. I shared a cabin with him at his suggestion and one of us was 'always awake on feet' throughout the boat at all times. Walt, at sea, was a fearless fighter. In port, he was a mild, kindly and even poetic type."

As mentioned previously, there were changes as well among crew members aboard *Billfish* after her initial run. Her commissioning XO, Gordon Selby, left to enter the prospective commanding officer (PCO) pool and later served with distinction aboard that submarine, the one with the decidedly problematic past. And, of course, among the other new crew members who came aboard for the boat's second run were Lieutenant Charlie Rush and Chief John Rendernick.

20 November 1943: 0615. Sighted BOWFIN bearing 160 [degrees] T, 4 miles.

0700. BOWFIN came close aboard and final arrangements for the conduct of the joint patrol were made by megaphone.

0720. Commenced joint surface patrol with BOWFIN, as follows:

Patrol origin: 11-00N; 112-00E.

Patrolling courses: 310 [degrees] T and 130 [degrees] T, reversing every two hours.

Scouting distance: 20 miles during daylight, 14 miles during darkness or low visibility.

Scouting speed: 9 knots during daylight; 7 knots during darkness.

Such a joint operation was nothing new. Several skippers and their commanders had explored having two submarines work together in close proximity, as *Bowfin* and *Billfish* were doing. While it cut down on the territory that they could patrol, it definitely allowed them to more effectively attack groups of targets. It also gave the ability for one submarine to offer a bit more protection for the other—to allow them to watch each other's back.

Of course, such a tandem required good coordination. Neither boat wanted to be caught behind a target when the other launched torpedoes in that general direction. It was also important to know always where the other boat was and what amount of cover fire and observation she could offer. It helped, too, if each captain had confidence in the other's abilities. However, like many things going on in the war at that time, the skippers had to make up the rules as they went along, learning from their mistakes, if they survived them. Then they could add those successful tactics to the "manual" in the process. At that time in the war, prospective submarine commanders and other crew members actually received copies of very recent war patrol reports and they dissected them in the classrooms in New London. What better submarine warfare textbook could there be than the actual details of what was going on at that very moment in the Pacific?

The sister submarines were able to use a new radio on this patrol, one that used voice transmissions and operated on a frequency at which the enemy was unlikely to hear them. That allowed them to use plain-language voice messages, not encrypted Morse code.

25 November 1943: 1305. Submerged to routine torpedoes and water battery. Too rough for this work on the surface for several days.

1826. Surfaced and headed north along the coast between Camranh Bay and Cape Varella. Position very much in doubt as have had no fix for 36 hours, but planned to make prearranged rendezvous with BOWFIN off Cape Varella at midnight.

Billfish did not have much luck finding potential targets over the next few days. According to the patrol logs, heavy seas and torrential rainstorms made it difficult for Lucas and his crew to line up their sights on any kind of target. That is, if they even happened to find one. At times, the submarine was quite literally lost, unable to rely on either celestial navigation or landmarks on the distant shore because of the dense clouds and pouring rain.

Billfish did run across a single ship early on the morning of November 25, first spying the vessel on radar off the port bow at a distance of ten thousand yards. They were attempting to rendezvous with *Bowfin* off Cape Varella. Captain Lucas was hesitant to try to maneuver around and stage any kind of attack on this vessel, though.

"It was still raining and visibility was poor," he later logged. "Decided to wait for daylight as firing blind was impracticable for the following reasons: (a) Possibility of contact being BOWFIN. (b) Radar indicated target was of small size and it was estimated that 15 feet was the minimum practicable depth setting in the existing heavy sea. Therefore worked for position ahead, but at daybreak the rain, which had showed signs of letting up, increased so that visibility was practically zero. Patrolled across the estimated track of the target using radar search but never regained contact."

Was Captain Lucas deliberately trying to avoid any confrontation with an enemy ship? Or was he merely being prudent, attempting to get back together with his sister submarine while waiting for better hunting weather?

They had exchanged radio communication with *Bowfin* at about nine p.m. the night before, so she was definitely in the area. Granted, weather conditions were bad. Griffith mentioned it in his patrol report, saying, "Do not consider that torpedoes would perform in this sea." Later, while trying to exchange information visually with *Billfish*, Griffith noted, "Seas so big that it was necessary to run before the wind to exchange searchlight signals at 500 yards, and then we could only see each other half the time."

Regardless, it now seemed to some of the crew that Lucas was once again fixated on the next rendezvous with their sister submarine to the exclusion of accomplishing anything else on this patrol.

No one on the bridge or in the conn said anything, but men exchanged glances. Whispers flared up again among the enlisted men, too, but the hissing ceased immediately anytime an officer approached.

Despite the bad weather and navigational difficulties that stymied *Billfish*, Griffith and *Bowfin* were having considerable success. Near the coast of Indochina, and in the midst of one of those blinding rainstorms that were giving Captain Lucas so much trouble, *Bowfin* suddenly found herself in the middle of an anthill of Japanese shipping. She almost collided head-on with a tanker. Griffith ordered all back, throwing the diesel engines into reverse.

"Pitch black and raining solid," Griffith wrote. "At first I thought I had blundered into the beach or some small islands although I had 75 fathoms of water. Came hard left to clear out to seaward and backed emergency to keep from ramming an enormous tanker."

With a quick run through the TDC data, tubes were readied and torpedoes were out of their tubes and on their way. She scored a direct hit and sank the 5,070-ton tanker *Ogurasan Maru*.

Now that their presence in the midst of the ships was known, Griffith could have been cautious, gone deep, and slipped away before it began hailing depth charges. Instead, he lined up on a second freighter and took out the 5,400-ton *Tainan Maru*.

"I figured this might be the biggest ship I would ever get to shoot," Griffith wrote. He also noted that it was raining so hard by then that it was extinguishing the gasoline fire that was burning on the sea's surface near the torpedoed ships. He also mentioned that one engine would not crank, the number ten torpedo door was jammed shut, and he had developed a huge blind spot in his radar, which explained the sub's popping up in the middle of the convoy without Griffith's knowing what it was.

Only a few hours later and while still being pounded by rain and rough seas, *Bowfin* was able to torpedo and sink a 690-ton coastal cargo ship, one of the many vessels that the Japanese had confiscated from the French plantation owners when they overran Indochina.

Meanwhile, Frederic Lucas and *Billfish* were still concentrating on looking for *Bowfin*, anxious to join up with their sister submarine. Despite the crew's excitement about bagging a target, none presented itself.

They wandered around in the foul weather, waiting.

CHAPTER TWELVE

BATTLE STATIONS!

"0300 BOWFIN *reported that she was in good position and asked permission to attack. Told her to go right ahead.*"

"0335 BOWFIN *reported that she only had two torpedoes left, suspected shell holes in her main induction, and was still in good position for an attack. Again told her to go right ahead.*"

—Logbook entries for USS *Billfish*, November 28, 1943

2 *7 November 1943: 1230. Passed through rendezvous and, not
making contact with BOWFIN, assumed that she would be
patrolling off Cape Varella. Set course for that position.*

*2100. (about) BOWFIN called on voice radio. Said approximate
position was off Cape Varella and that she would head north 7-8
miles off coast. Replied that we were coming in on Cape Varella from
the eastward and would remain to seaward of her track. Exchanged
other information.*

It was early on the morning of the twenty-eigth. *Billfish* was
patrolling on the surface. Charlie Rush had the watch. Only he
and Captain Lucas were on the bridge at the time.

The rain had slackened to little more than a drizzle and it was
dark, a perfect night for a predator like *Billfish* to hunt its prey.
Their view was restricted, but so was the enemy's. The submarine's
radar was superior, too.

The call came up the hatch from below that radar had spotted
five contacts, all at about 290 degrees and at a distance of about
eight miles. An electric charge ran up and down the boat.

Rush gave the order to turn to that heading and work for position at about eighteen knots. There was no radar sweep detected from the target convoy, indicating they likely had none. If they had it, they would almost certainly be using it in weather like this. And in a part of the sea where American submarines were doing real damage.

"Battle stations!" Lucas called, and the ship jumped to action, ready to make a charge at the contacts steaming along the surface in the far distance.

Perfect! Dark, rainy night, a tightly packed enemy convoy with no radar, no reason to suspect an imminent attack from escorts, and *Billfish* had no reason to suspect the ships had any idea they were already in *Billfish*'s sights.

Rush felt a quickening of his pulse and relished the feel of the damp air and wind on his face as the submarine made good speed on the surface toward a prime firing point.

Finally, after all the frustrations of this disappointing run so far, they were now in a good position to do some serious damage to the enemy. *Billfish* was about to cease being a target, cowering on the bottom, and start shooting back for a change!

The rush of adrenaline took the young officer back to *Thresher*. He could not help but think what "Moke" Millican would do in a situation like this, what the look on his face would be as they rushed across the wave tops to get into position to make a full-blown attack, using every weapon in their arsenal.

Just then, the radar operator reported brief flashes of another vessel's radar, but based on frequency, it appeared to be from an American ship. They quickly surmised it was *Bowfin*, on the other side of the convoy, between their position and the shore near Cape Varella. They, too, were bombarding the convoy with their radio waves. And they, too, were likely primed for the attack.

They were about to catch the Japanese in a wicked set of pincers!

As soon as the *Billfish* crew felt they had an accurate set of details on the convoy—course, speed, composition—they raised *Bowfin* on the newly installed radio circuit to see if she was seeing the same thing they were.

"Nope," Griffith replied.

Bowfin had no contacts on their scope at all. They had not yet seen those beautiful target vessels that *Billfish* still had painted all over her radar scope.

Rush tensed, ready to hear the commands from his captain that would send them maneuvering for an attack. Instead, Lucas calmly instructed the radio operator to give the other submarine the position, course, and speed estimate of the Japanese ships in the convoy, as well as to make certain he gave them *Billfish*'s position as well.

Then radar picked up two more vessels, smaller and moving more quickly. Patrol boats, most likely. Escorts for the convoy. No surprise there.

Then they could hear weakly the enemy's sonar as it began pinging. No reason to think that the Japanese knew the two submarines were out there, ready to tighten the vise on them. They were still too far away. The escorts were simply scanning randomly as a matter of course, making certain there were no American sharks in the water ahead.

Still, the *ping! ping! ping!* was a familiar, startling reminder to all of them of the horrible night of thunder they had spent submerged, steaming in a straight line, in the Makassar Strait.

0300. (about) BOWFIN reported that she was in good position and asked permission to attack. Told her to go right ahead. She was on the inshore side with an excellent land mass and cloud background. We were unfortunately on the opposite side with a bright clear sky (the first in many days) in the background. We were also on the outside track as the convoy rounded Cape Varella.

"Captain, Bowfin wants to know if you have any problem with them going ahead and attacking from their position."

Lucas did not hesitate.

"Tell them to go right ahead."

Charlie Rush, standing at the elbow of his skipper, blinked hard. Yes, there were good reasons for them to allow Bowfin to take the lead on this. But would Lucas stand back and let Griffith and his guys have all the fun?

This was supposed to be a coordinated attack, after all. Not a one-boat show.

"Coordinated" surely did not mean telling the sister submarine to wade in while Billfish lingered back, ten thousand yards away, too far to shoot torpedoes, out of harm's way.

Then Captain Lucas gave a simple, innocuous-sounding order. It shocked everyone in the crew who heard it, even as each man moved quickly to make it happen.

"Turn to heading one-two-oh, maintain eighteen knots."

What was he thinking? Though they were already nearly six miles away from the convoy, he was turning, running in the opposite direction from the fight, and he was doing it just about as fast as the submarine would go!

0317-19. Observed and heard at least five torpedo explosions as BOWFIN attacked. This was followed by gunfire, searchlights, and a few random depth charges. BOWFIN then reported the results of her attack as one sunk, two damaged and said she would wait for us. Also reported the two undamaged ships standing down toward us, 4-5000 yards apart. Commenced approach on the one to *seaward. They had increased speed and were zig-zagging radically and independently.*

Rush could not hold his tongue.

"Captain, you can't do this. This is wrong."

"What do you mean, Mr. Rush?"

"You can't take off like this. There are more targets still afloat, and *Bowfin* might need us."

Rush knew he had once again trod on quicksand. He had just questioned the decisions of the captain of a warship. His commander.

Men could be shot by a firing squad for such insubordination in a combat situation.

"No, you're right. You're right, Mr. Rush. Turn to heading two-eight-zero. Maintain speed. Eighteen knots. We will try to get a shot on the seaward target."

Rush swallowed hard. He hoped the men in the shears above them or anyone else on the boat had not heard the brief exchange. Had not heard the young officer question the orders and discretion of a captain who had a dozen years in submarines. Or, arguably even worse, heard their captain make a foolish call, and then, when challenged by a junior officer, reverse it.

Then Rush concentrated on the job at hand, getting lined up to finish the attack on those remaining ships out there as they scattered and tried to run away from them. Now that he had convinced his captain to do the right thing, they needed to make the most of it.

0335. (about) BOWFIN reported that she only had two torpedoes left, suspected shell holes in her main induction, and was still in good position for an attack. Again told her to go right ahead.

The 287 boat was about out of bullets. She had also suffered damage from a deck gun on one of the ships she was attacking. She was wounded in the main induction line and that was leaking, causing flooding. That was a potentially serious situation if she could not stay on the surface long enough to repair the damage.

Still, so long as he was afloat, Walt Griffith wanted to fight on, to shoot until he had nothing else for the enemy.

Frederic Lucas radioed that it was fine with him for *Bowfin* to go ahead and press the attack. Again, considering their relative positions, that was likely the correct call. Griffith did so, firing his last two torpedoes. One exploded prematurely, only five hundred yards after leaving the tube. That deflected the other fish and sent it spinning off onto a new course, causing it to miss its target.

"This premature cost me a 7,000 ton vessel and two sure hits," Griffith later complained in his report.

Meanwhile, as *Bowfin* pressed the attack, Captain Lucas told his own crew again to reverse course and flee the area.

Charlie Rush pounded the rail of the bridge with the heel of his hand.

"Captain, you cannot do this! You have to turn around and go get those scattered targets! Or at least stay close by to assist *Bowfin*. She has damage and can't submerge without risking going down."

"I can't do it," Lucas said sadly, quietly, his head down. Rush could hardly hear the words over the full-bore rumbling of their engines and the wind in his ears, but they were unmistakable. "I can't do it."

"I can," Rush said. "Let me do it."

Lucas looked at him then, his face blank, emotionless.

"You know I cannot turn over command of my ship, Mr. Rush," he replied, his voice flat and hollow and almost swept away by the wind and the throbbing diesels.

"I don't want command, Captain. I just want the conn."

"I can't do that. I can't do that." Lucas turned and looked away, gazing back behind them, to where billows of smoke and the dull glow of a small fire marked the hell *Bowfin* had just raised in that section of ocean.

Then Lucas moved a step closer to the younger man and looked him squarely in the eye.

"Mr. Rush, I promise you, when we get back to squadron, I will resign from submarines."

It was the first time the captain had looked his junior officer in the eye in days. It was clear this move was not impulsive. Frederic Lucas had been giving his next maneuver some serious thought.

"I promise you this. I will resign from submarines when we return home."

Charlie Rush was stunned. He could not believe what his captain had just promised him. Nor could he believe the next words out of his own mouth.

"Captain, you do that . . . you leave submarines . . . and I will not tell anybody about what has happened on this run. I promise you. . . ."

At that moment, one of *Bowfin*'s last two torpedoes, the one nudged aside by the premature fish, exploded at end-of-run. It was close enough to *Billfish* when it did so that it gave the boat a solid wallop and all those topside a good soaking.

That blast effectively cut off the small, intense drama that was playing out on the submarine's bridge.

In a way, Rush was relieved. The last thing he wanted to do was to talk with Navy brass about what had happened. He had witnesses, and he was confident they would back up his account of the way things had unfolded on board *Billfish*. Still, any such revelations would not only reflect badly on two of his superior officers but on the entire submarine service. Worse transgressions had gone unreported because they involved the character or judgment of fellow submariners. The brotherhood was close, solid, and always reluctant to put anyone who was a member of it in a bad light, regardless of his sin.

Over the next three hours, *Billfish*'s deck log details a series of maneuvers supposedly attempting to get them into position for a shot at one of the ships that had managed to escape the wrath of *Bowfin*. At least one of them could well have been damaged in the attack and would seem to be an easy target.

At one point, just after five a.m., *Billfish* did manage to line up and fire four torpedoes on a target. They whooshed away in numerical order from each of the stern tubes at a distance the report described as about thirty-six hundred yards—just over two miles.

"Heard and felt one torpedo explosion which timed with correct torpedo run but target was then obscured by smoke from our engines as we went ahead for daylight position," Lucas wrote in his patrol report.

She did not get close enough or have a good enough angle to make another attack. Finally, assuming the fleeing contacts had gone in too close to shore for the submarine to pursue safely, *Billfish* called off the chase. Again, it is not far-fetched to say that this was the intelligent thing to do. The weather had broken and the rain stopped. Visibility was better. Antisubmarine forces would be much more prevalent closer to land, along with other swift and deadly patrol craft. A submarine's options are also limited greatly near shore and shallower water.

Griffith called in to report that he was headed out to sea so he could make repairs to the bullet-riddled induction piping. Then, with no torpedoes to shoot and most of the ammunition for his deck guns expended in the direction of those enemy ships, he reported that he would set a course toward home port. He was now officially toothless. He would now leave the hunting to *Billfish*.

"Wish I had 24 more torpedoes," Walt Griffith wrote in his log. *1845. Surfaced and set course to the eastward.*

Charlie Rush tried to keep his mind on his job when he was on watch. When he was off duty, in his cramped bunk, even as tired as he was, he had difficulty finding sleep.

If they lived to make it back to Fremantle, would Lucas keep his promise to leave submarines? Or would Admiral Christie even allow him to quit if he submitted his resignation? Christie liked Lucas. He was one of his favorite skippers. That was obvious. He had given *Billfish* a "successful" on her first patrol, awarded them the Submarine Combat Patrol Insignia, and congratulated them for their "assist" to *Bowfin*.

All that, and Lucas and his boat had not sunk a duck on that run.

But the real question that nagged at the young lieutenant was this: If Lucas reneged, if he changed his mind or if he was not able to talk the admiral into letting him go, what would Rush do then?

Would he keep quiet about what had happened on *Billfish*'s second war patrol and, possibly, sail with Lucas again? Or would he risk it all and tell people about the events of the night of November 11? Of the captain's dangerous lapses in leadership and judgment while working with *Bowfin* in the South China Sea?

Charlie Rush was convinced the lives of the crew members of *Billfish* — or whatever boat Frederic Lucas commanded next — could hang in the balance.

CHAPTER THIRTEEN

A GENTLEMEN'S AGREEMENT

"The material condition and state of cleanliness of the ship, and the morale of the ship's company, is excellent and bespeaks a high state of battle efficiency which it is felt will be amply demonstrated when opportunity finally presents itself to come to grips with the enemy."

—J. M. Haines, commander of Task Group Seventy-one Point Three, writing in First Endorsement to the patrol report of the second war patrol of USS *Billfish*, December 24, 1943

"This patrol is considered successful for purpose of award of the Submarine Combat Insignia."

—Admiral R. W. Christie, commander of Task Force Seventy-one, writing in Second Endorsement to the patrol report of the second war patrol of USS *Billfish*, December 24, 1943

The remainder of *Billfish*'s second run was not without incident. On December 8, while the boat was patrolling on the surface in rough seas, an especially high wave swept one of the officers, Ensign F. A. Ryan, off the deck and into the water. Fortunately, the incident was witnessed as it happened, but within a brief moment Ryan was pulled hundreds of yards away from the moving submarine.

The young officer wore heavy, woolen foul-weather gear. It soaked up the seawater and it was all he could do to stay afloat while the submarine stopped and turned around to go back and try to pick him up. Max Ostrander tied himself to the submarine's deck with a line and went overboard to try to help his shipmate. With heroic effort, he reached Ryan just as he ran out of strength. Somehow, despite the tossing of the sea, Ostrander managed to keep Ryan's head above the waves as he pulled him back to the boat.

Both men were unharmed.

On the morning of December 14, *Billfish* negotiated the Celebes Sea on the way back to Australia. Radar spotted an aerial contact at eight miles and the diving officer ordered them to submerge. A lookout spotted the airplane just as he ducked down the hatch. Even though they quickly went to two hundred feet, then on down to more than 350 feet, two bombs exploded close enough to rattle their teeth and once again recall some unpleasant recent history.

Then, despite not hearing even a hint of turning screws or sonar pinging to indicate the presence of any surface vessels, about eight depth charges exploded around them. Fortunately, none of them was close enough to bother anything other than the crew's already frayed nerves.

They could only surmise the airplane dropped the charges.

In the "Remarks" section at the end of his official patrol report for *Billfish*'s second run, Captain Frederic Lucas devoted two long sentences to the summation of his joint patrol with *Bowfin*.

No opportunity was had to conclusively test the effectiveness of the joint patrol due to lack of contacts in the open sea where full advantage of the surface chase could be taken. On the occasion of the one contact when the two submarines were in contact BOWFIN completed a highly successful attack and expended the last of her torpedoes, but after one attack we were forced to submerge before obtaining satisfactory position for further attacks by the coming of daylight and the proximity of the shore and anti-submarine craft and aircraft.

The only other comments about the joint patrol dealt with the effectiveness of the new VHF radio system that they used to coordinate.

Though she had steamed almost thirteen thousand miles on her second patrol, and burned over a hundred thousand gallons of diesel fuel in the process, *Billfish* returned to squadron headquarters with twenty of her initial twenty-four torpedoes still on the racks and in the tubes in the aft and forward torpedo rooms.

Regardless, Admiral Ralph Waldo Christie, the commander of Task Force Seventy-one, said in his endorsement of the patrol:

For the greater part of the time in Area the BILLFISH was handicapped by extremely bad weather which unquestionably hampered making contacts in an area normally productive of torpedo targets. On the one occasion of contact with a convoy, BILLFISH, as in her First Patrol, was destined to coach the BOWFIN on and be left with no targets in a favorable attack position. This excellent cooperation was instrumental in the infliction of tremendous damage on the enemy without the stimulating pleasure of having actually fired the torpedoes that did the work.

This patrol is considered successful for purpose of award of the Submarine Combat Insignia.

The Force Commander congratulates the Commanding Officer, Officers and Crew on their "Assist" to the BOWFIN and for inflicting the following damage on the enemy:

DAMAGED

1 AK (UNIDENTIFIED)——6,000 tons

John Meade Haines, the commander of Task Group Seventy-one Point Three, was equally as understanding of the lack of results by *Billfish* and her crew. In his remarks, he said:

The coverage of these [patrol areas in enemy-controlled waters] although unfruitful was thorough and deserving of better results. Particular note is taken of the manner in which contact information furnished by the BILLFISH was capitalized upon by the BOWFIN, even though the former was unable from her position to profit by the contact.

The material condition and state of cleanliness of the ship, and the morale of the ship's company, is excellent and bespeaks a high state of battle efficiency which it is felt will be amply demonstrated when opportunity finally presents itself to come to grips with the enemy.

So his bosses were fine with how Captain Lucas ran war patrol number two aboard *Billfish*.

If they were satisfied with Lucas and *Billfish*, they were absolutely thrilled with *Bowfin* and Griffith. Christie termed that submarine's second run "the classic of all submarine patrols." She received credit from the squadron commander for sinking a total of fourteen vessels, the largest haul for any patrol up to that point in the war. After the ultraconservative postwar estimates were completed, the run still ended up with five official kills, and tied for sixth-most-productive patrol based on number of ships sunk.

That's not all: Christie awarded Griffith a Navy Cross. He also gave his XO, William Thompson, a Silver Star and proclaimed him ready for command of his own boat. But to top it off, when Christie's cocker spaniel had puppies, the admiral named one of them "Bowfin."

When *Billfish* arrived back in port, Charlie Rush did not stick around to see if Lucas kept his promise to resign from submarines. He promptly put in for two weeks' leave. He bought a ticket for Adelaide, over twenty-five hundred miles away from Fremantle and Perth. He knew there would be no Navy people there on Australia's southern coast and that was precisely what he wanted. He dreaded facing the question "So, how was your last run?"

While Rush was half a continent away, Frederic C. Lucas Jr., class of 1930, U.S. Naval Academy, turned in his resignation from submarine command and requested surface-ship duty. According to some accounts, Lucas requested a private talk with Christie. He told his commander that he had never felt comfortable at the helm of a submarine and that was compounded many times over in a war situation. He also confessed that his discomfort had adversely affected his ability to do his duty.

While admitting no loss of control or failure to lead, and not sharing any of the details of the just-completed patrol, Lucas told Christie that he felt he was not doing justice to his submarine or its crew. He suggested that his command be given to one of the several experienced officers then in Fremantle, anxiously awaiting the opportunity to assume the helm of a boat.

Christie shared the conversation with no one, but wrote of it briefly in a diary he kept.

"I am obliged to detach Lucas from command of *Billfish* at his own request. He is convinced that he is temperamentally unsuited for submarine command. I have been quite well satisfied with him although he has had two unproductive patrols. However, based on that, I would not have removed him."

Lucas went directly to Brisbane for a staff position at Squadron Eight. Ironically, he did briefly helm another submarine during the war. USS *Caiman* (SS-323) was on her first war patrol in late November 1944 when her commissioning skipper became ill and put into Saipan. Lucas was dispatched to complete the patrol and bring the boat and crew to Fremantle, arriving in mid-January 1945. Despite two attempted attacks, *Caiman* did not damage or sink any enemy ships on that patrol and the squadron commander stated that "results were not successful for purpose of award of the Submarine Combat Insignia."

Lucas went on to serve as commander of two surface ships, the USS *Graffias* (AF-29), a supply or "stores" ship, and USS *Shenandoah* (AD-26), a destroyer tender. He later had tours of duty at the Bureau of Naval Personnel and Office of the Chief of Naval Operations, then went back to sea duty in 1956 as captain of USS *Los Angeles* (CA-135), a World War II–era heavy cruiser. He and his crew aboard *Los Angeles* received a letter of commendation for their work with the Regulus missile project. After a tour of duty as group commander, fleet training group, San Diego, he retired from the Navy in 1960.

As skipper of *Billfish*, he held the rank of lieutenant commander. He later received promotions to commander, then to captain.

From all indications, he served with distinction at each post after leaving *Billfish*. According to all reports, those who served with him liked and respected him and considered him a fine officer.

Captain Frederic C. Lucas passed away in February 2000 and was interred in Arlington National Cemetery in Washington, D.C., on March 9 of that year.

When Charlie Rush returned to Fremantle from his two-week leave in Adelaide, he learned that *Billfish* had a new skipper, Vernon Clark Turner, a native of Brownwood, Texas, and a graduate of the Naval Academy class of 1933.

Captain Lucas had kept their gentlemen's agreement, a pact made in a most unlikely place—on the bridge of a submarine in the middle of a surface attack. The young submarine officer was relieved. Now Rush could keep his end of the bargain. He would tell no one the details about what happened aboard *Billfish* during that harrowing run.

At least, not until almost sixty years later.

Even then it took a nagging omission, one that he felt had to be corrected, to finally cause him to break the silence, to reveal the true story of what happened that night beneath the surface of Makassar Strait.

CHAPTER FOURTEEN

TO HONOR A FRIEND

"Without courage, you might as well not be in it. You've got to have courage—moral courage, physical courage—and honor. Honor means telling the truth even when it might not be to your advantage."

—Retired Captain Charles W. Rush Jr., *Billfish* officer and Navy Cross recipient, when asked to give advice to members of today's submarine service

USS *Billfish* completed four more war patrols under Lieutenant Commander Vernon Turner and two more while skippered by Lieutenant Commander L. C. Farley. In her eight runs, she claimed six vessels sunk, but postwar official count lowered that to three, for about forty-three hundred tons. She went out of commission in 1946. Then, after years in mothballs, she became a training vessel for the Naval Reserve in Boston from 1960 to 1968. She ultimately was stricken from the Navy's registry of ships on April Fool's Day 1968, and the Navy sold her remains for scrap.

Her sister submarine, USS *Bowfin*, completed nine patrols and was preparing for her tenth when she got word the war had ended. She claimed to have sunk or damaged fifty-four enemy vessels, over 176,000 tons, though the official tally was sixteen sunk for sixty-eight hundred tons. She received the Navy Unit Citation for her service, which included all those ships sent to the bottom, laying mines, rescuing downed pilots, and supplying Philippine guerrillas.

However, this much-honored submarine was also involved—

unknowingly—in one of the real tragedies of World War II. In August 1944, she sank an unmarked Japanese cargo ship, the *Tsushima Maru*. *Bowfin's* crew had no way of knowing the ship carried over eight hundred children. The Japanese were evacuating them from Okinawa ahead of the anticipated invasion of that island by the Allies.

Seven hundred and sixty-seven of the children died in the attack.

Today, the *Bowfin*, "the Pearl Harbor Avenger," is a museum ship, open to the public, at Pearl Harbor, Hawaii, not far from the memorial for the battleship USS *Arizona*. She became a National Historic Landmark in 1986.

Today visitors to *Bowfin* have the opportunity to see episodes of the classic television series *The Silent Service* playing in the museum's minitheater. An episode that features *Bowfin* is screened every hour on the hour. It depicts the experience of a young officer named John Bertrand on *Bowfin's* third patrol—Walt Griffith's second at the helm and the run just after its joint operation with *Billfish*—and is titled "The Seasick Texas Submariner." Bertrand wrote the script for that episode, which gives visitors an excellent look at what life was like aboard those boats.

Charlie Rush made one more run on *Billfish*, then got orders to return to Portsmouth, New Hampshire. There he was to help put a new *Balao*-class submarine, the USS *Sea Owl* (SS-405), into commission. That boat went on to perform some of the early tests of a new acoustic torpedo—nicknamed "Cutie"—and had some success in sinking enemy ships before the war ended.

After a brief time at war on *Sea Owl*, Rush was assigned to the Bureau of Ordnance (BUORD) at the Navy Department in Washington, D.C. His job there was to help build a new, high-speed torpedo for submarines. He also served as executive officer on USS

Carbonero (SS-337) from June 1948 to July 1951, and later commanded USS *Queenfish* (SS-393) from 1952 to 1954, including taking her to war during the Korean conflict.

He was a popular skipper with his crew. Cliff Hoxsey, who served under Rush on *Queenfish*, says, "In my twenty-one years in the service, I never served under any officer who came close to matching him. It's true that we went where we weren't supposed to be doing reconnaissance sometimes. But he was an outstanding commander."

Later, while working in the U.S. Navy Office of Operations, he made recommendations that led to one of history's most significant accomplishments, the successful under-ice voyage of USS *Nautilus* from the Pacific to the Atlantic by way of the North Pole in 1958. His boss at the time, Admiral I. J. Galantin, was so proud of Rush's contribution to that historic passage that he took the unusual step of issuing a memo to be placed in Rush's service file, to be considered when he came up for promotion. In that memo, Galantin wrote, "In late 1956 when the undersigned was Head, Submarine Warfare Branch, Office of Chief of Naval Operations, the then Commander Charles W. Rush, Jr., as Head of the Submarine Weapons System Section (OP-311E) recommended to me that USS NAUTILUS (SS(N) 571) make a transarctic passage. To the best of my knowledge, the concept of such a transit from ocean to ocean across the northern route was completely original; it had never been suggested before. After your preliminary work substantiated the feasibility of your plan, I authorized you to discuss it with Commander William R. Anderson, U.S. Navy, who was then slated to take command of NAUTILUS . . . the vision and initiative shown in your original proposal were instrumental in the successful planning and execution of this historic naval accomplishment."

Rush was also instrumental in the development of the UUM-44

SUBROC submarine weapons system and worked on other guided-missile weapons that were specifically designed to be fired from submarines. Along the way, compliments of the Navy, he received an education at Caltech. He retired from the Navy in 1961 after twenty years of service and worked in aviation and as a consultant for ocean systems and in submarine safety.

The other key players in the drama below the Makassar Strait that Armistice Day went about their business as well. Amazingly, no one ever spoke of the events of that night, of what really happened. Or at least not to anyone in a position to do something about it.

That is the Navy way, of course. And especially the submariner's way. They lived. They made it back to home port. The skipper, the XO, and the other officer who "cracked" moved to other duty and performed well, defending their country. No need to talk about it.

Besides, if the truth came out, it would reflect negatively on submarines and submariners. There was no need for that.

But one thing nagged at Charlie Rush, even as he excelled in life after *Billfish* and after the Navy. The men who helped him save the boat that night, because of their silence and loyalty, had never been properly recognized for what they had done. Still, he was not sure how to reopen the incident without reopening an old wound at the same time.

He decided to let it lie.

Jump forward fifty-eight years, to the new millennium. It was over Mexican food and beers and a conversation with an old friend that the wheels were set in motion, not only for three heroes to be honored but for this remarkable story of their courage to come to light.

Charlie Rush was visiting an old Navy buddy and Annapolis classmate in California one night, swapping sea stories. For one of the few times since it occurred, Rush told someone else the basics of the tale.

The "buddy" was John E. "Jack" Bennett, another hero of World War II. Bennett was a young officer aboard USS *San Francisco* (CA-38), a heavy cruiser that was involved in what Fleet Admiral Ernest J. King described as "the most vicious sea battle fought in history." In that clash off Guadalcanal in November 1942, eighteen hundred American sailors—including two admirals—died and six U.S. ships were sunk, most by battleships and Japanese dive-bombers. Four men received the Medal of Honor—two of them posthumously—for their actions in that battle. Twenty-nine others—twenty of them posthumously—received the Navy Cross.

Bennett was one of the Navy Cross recipients, and many of the other honors were the result of citations he wrote and submitted. And most of those citations were based on the courageous actions he witnessed firsthand on the burning decks of the *San Francisco*. Bennett was determined that men receive the recognition due them for their actions in battle.

Still, despite all he had seen in war, he was amazed at the *Billfish* story. Amazed and intrigued about it to the point that he soon became just as determined as Charlie Rush to see that the right thing was finally done.

As it happened, John Rendernick resided in a town in California not far from where Bennett lived. Rush suggested his friend give Rendernick a call and talk with him about the incident. He did, and the more he heard, the more Rendernick's version of the story backed up Rush's, the more Bennett was convinced that these men deserved proper recognition. However, Bennett also felt strongly that any acknowledgment include his classmate and friend Charlie Rush.

He e-mailed Rush: "Charlie, I think you deserve the Medal of

Honor, but after all this time, I think we would be unwise to go that route. I am going to turn in a citation for you for a Navy Cross."

Rush, who wanted nothing to get in the way of a medal for Rendernick and a citation for Charley Odom, protested, but Bennett went ahead anyway. Meanwhile, Rush wrote a citation for Chief Rendernick to receive a Silver Star. That and the one Bennett prepared for Rush were submitted jointly.

Now it was the Navy red tape that stalled the telling of a wonderful story and the long-overdue recognition for a couple of bona fide heroes. In the Navy's rules that govern how citations are to be awarded, Rule 1A requires that the actions of the person who is to receive a reward must be witnessed by a senior officer. While Rush was Rendernick's senior officer, the captain and the other two senior men aboard *Billfish* who oversaw Rush had since passed away. There was no one left to vouch for what Charlie Rush had done in those hours of peril.

He did not hesitate.

"Just withdraw the joint citation and let's resubmit for Chief Rendernick," he told Bennett. So that was what they did.

But somewhere in the depths of the Office of the Chief of Naval Operations, an active-duty naval aviator named Jeffery Campbell had been watching the joint citation wend its way through channels. He was shocked when a technicality appeared to be about to sink a most deserving award. Campbell had on his desk a detailed statement from John Rendernick, another from the engineman, Charley Odom, and a third from the chief of the boat, Emmett Carpenter. To Campbell's way of thinking, the statements of three chief petty officers equaled at least one statement from a senior officer.

Rush would later hear that Campbell was about to retire from the Navy, and he told his colleagues that he intended to do something about this injustice right before he went out. Even though it violated Rule 1A, Campbell revived Charlie Rush's Navy Cross citation and pushed it through.

In January 2002, President George W. Bush awarded Charlie Rush the Navy Cross. Rush did not actually receive the medal until April. Rear Admiral Paul F. Sullivan, director of the Submarine Warfare Division, represented Secretary of the Navy Gordon England in a ceremony held at Memorial Hall at the U.S. Naval Academy in Annapolis. On one wall was a huge banner with Captain James Lawrence's famous dying command from the War of 1812, "Don't give up the ship."

The text of the citation that accompanied Rush's Navy Cross was read aloud to those assembled there. Near the end, it said, "Captain Rush's inspiring and exceptional performance of duty under the worst imaginable conditions and in the face of seemingly certain death were directly responsible for saving BILLFISH and all hands from loss and for restoring the shattered confidence of the crew. By his courageous actions, superb leadership, and loyal dedication to duty, Captain Rush reflected great credit upon himself and upheld the highest traditions of the United States Naval Service."

Fittingly, the award recognized the courage and ingenuity of Rush and his shipmates, not the shortcomings of others. The words were carefully chosen in the citation. Rush would have it no other way. "When an extremely severe depth charge attack incapacitated the Captain and all officers senior to Captain Rush [then Lieutenant Rush], with cool courage and outstanding professionalism he directed the damage control efforts directly responsible for saving the ship."

During the ceremony, Rush looked out over the audience and saw the faces of several of his Academy classmates. He also saw a few of the surviving crew members who were aboard *Billfish* that horrible night. Indeed, there are only a few of them left.

"I was not alone the night of the depth-charge attack," he said. "And I'm not alone today."

However, one shipmate—and a major player in the incident— was conspicuously missing from the audience in Annapolis that day.

Chief John Rendernick had died—gone on "eternal patrol," as the submariners say—the previous December. He knew he was to receive the Silver Star, but he did not live to actually touch it, to show it to his family and friends.

The citation that accompanied his Silver Star described the extraordinary actions Rendernick took to save the boat. It concluded by saying, "By his cool and courageous actions, exceptional initiative, and loyal dedication to duty, Chief Petty Officer Rendernick reflected great credit upon himself and upheld the highest traditions of the United States Naval Service."

The Silver Star is the third-highest military decoration that can be awarded to a member of the Armed Forces, and is typically given for gallantry in action.

In June 2002, Chief Engineman Charley Odom received from Admiral Sullivan a special commendation recognizing his actions during the depth-charge attack.

After a brief account of the miracles he worked on *Billfish*, Odom's commendation says, "Chief Odom's courageous actions and loyal dedication to duty reflected great credit upon himself and upheld the highest traditions of the United States Naval Service."

In August 2004, in a special ceremony held at Pearl Harbor, Hawaii, Chief Rendernick received another significant recognition. The Damage Control Wet Trainer facility was renamed in his honor.

Admiral Sullivan was there for that ceremony as well and

said, "This is a great occasion to honor a man of courage and a true patriot, and really exemplifies what a chief petty officer is all about."

Master Chief Michael Benko proudly represented chief petty officers at the ceremony and said, "It is the officers that take the ship into battle, but it is the chief petty officers that run the ship. We are witnesses today to Chief Rendernick and his efforts to lead his men in saving USS *Billfish*."

It took almost sixty years, but some of the heroes of *Billfish* finally received their due. It is unclear whether this is the first time a Navy Cross, a Silver Star, and a rear admiral's citation have ever been awarded for actions that, according to the official patrol report, never happened.

The author has been unable to find any other citations that have been awarded for actions that occurred so long before.

However, one thing is for sure. Their story has finally been told.

EPILOGUE

"Say not, 'I have found the truth,' but rather,
'I have found a truth.'"

—Kahlil Gibran

War inevitably gives men and women the opportunity to demonstrate courage. Whether it is in a foxhole, on a beach, in the air over enemy territory, aboard a ship, or in a submarine, routine bravery occurs often. Exceptional bravery is sometimes recognized, sometimes not.

The highest award for courage in the U.S. military is the Congressional Medal of Honor—established originally to recognize valor among members of the U.S. Navy—and more than thirty-four hundred men have received it. So has one woman, Mary Walker, for action at Bull Run on July 21, 1861.

Other medals, usually service-specific, are also awarded for those who demonstrate exceptional valor, above and beyond the call of duty. This includes the Navy Cross, the second-highest recognition, the equivalent of the Army's Distinguished Service Cross and the Air Force Cross. As of this writing, and since its inception in 1919, just over 6,375 men have been awarded the Navy Cross.

The Silver Star is the third-highest award, and can be awarded to a member of any branch of the American Armed Forces. Since Congress created it in 1918, more than one hundred thousand of these medals have been given, but that number may be misleading. Colonel David Hackworth received ten of them himself for service in Korea and Vietnam. Still, considering the number of men and women who have served, it is a prestigious and notable honor.

There is a corollary, though, to the statement about war giving individuals the chance to demonstrate bravery. It also exposes those who are not up to the task.

Who among us would have shown the bravery and clearheadedness of Charles Rush when he took the conn of *Billfish* and successfully guided her from beneath those who so determinedly hunted her? Would we have performed as John D. Rendernick did when he took charge of the damage control party and led them to extraordinary measures to keep their submarine functioning? And could any of us say we would have been able to ignore the thunder of almost continual depth charges—knowing the next blast could let loose the flood of inrushing seawater—and perform our jobs the way Chief Charley T. Odom did? The way practically all the rest of the crew of the submarine did in November 1943?

Or would we have cracked?

In 2002, about the time the real story of that day aboard *Billfish* finally emerged, a reporter asked Charlie Rush a loaded question. Why did the captain's official patrol report covering those awful hours tell a story so different from what actually happened? I have asked him the same question.

Even then, nearly six decades later, Rush was hesitant to talk about it.

"There's no need to get into that," he told the reporter. "The citation says the senior officers were incapacitated. Why get into anything more?"

In an article he wrote for *Polaris*, a publication dedicated to World War II submarine history, Charley Odom says, "In combat, there are many surprises. Personality traits come to the fore. One's own behavior might bring unexpected bravery or unexpected fear. Men who had been shipmates for years found it almost impossible to believe one reacted in a specific manner. Cover was stripped away. Some hard rock toughs wilted temporarily while meeker shipmates might become leaders. Men who face death together are more tolerant of each other. We were thankful that we had control over fear and rage."

We will never know how John Rendernick felt about it. At the ceremony at Pearl Harbor at which the training facility received his name, his daughter, Mary Kay Rendernick, said her father spoke little of his submarine experiences, and certainly never said anything about the depth-charge attack.

"He was a very secretive man in his day," she said. "He did not talk about being in the military too often."

She was surprised when she got the call from the Navy that he was to be honored with the naming of the training facility at Pearl Harbor and that she was invited to be there. She knew nothing about the events of that night or her father's heroism in the Makassar Strait.

"I am amazed that he was chosen. If he were alive today, he would be overwhelmed. He said the submarine force is unique, unlike any other job. He called the old submarines 'cigars under the sea.'"

Odom still is reluctant to talk about the specifics. He points out that he was back in the aft torpedo room, in the maneuvering room, working the whole time. He knew little of what was going on in the control room or conning tower.

When pressed by the reporter back in 2002—and by this author later—Charlie Rush finally elaborated. I suspect it was the reminder we both gave him, that today's young sailor or soldier should know the entire story of what happened to the men who went before them when they marched, flew, or steamed off to war.

"He cracked," Rush ultimately said, in his forceful, direct manner. "The skipper simply lost it. The third officer required sedation. Men crack. The XO was exhausted, burned-out. We were running out of air. Each of these men went on to service elsewhere and served with honor."

Then he told me, "When a man assumes command of other men, you do not crack. But men are only human beings."

When I speak with other submariners and talk about the *Billfish*, I get a reaction very similar to Rush's. It is almost as if talking about any lack of get-it-done tenacity, letting the world know about any demonstrated lack of courage, is not allowed in a service that thrives on silence. One that is such a closed brotherhood that watches over its own against any NQPs — "nonqualified personnel," those who have not been baptized and confirmed, "qualified in submarines," and allowed to wear the dolphins.

Rush as much as admits it.

"When we got back to Fremantle, I certainly would have been justified in filing charges of cowardice in the face of the enemy on two of my brother submariners. But after spending a few weeks in Adelaide, resting, walking on the beach, I came to a conclusion. Why file charges? Who would it help? Would it help win the war? Would it help the ship? The men? Me? No. I let it go. When I got back, the captain had moved on. Not a man on the crew ever said a word. That is how the Navy works."

The Navy and the submarine service.

When asked specifically about how he now views his captain, Charlie Rush says, "There was never any bad blood between us. I felt sympathy for his having been thrust into a position he really was not capable of handling. I certainly did not dislike him."

Indeed, Rush blames the higher brass in the U.S. Navy for placing men who were unprepared or ill trained at the helms of submarines that were destined for war.

Politics? Lack of foresight? Desperation? Whatever it was, it put men into situations where they were more likely to fail, and if they did, it could have cost good men their lives.

"I found it inexcusable that they would put officers — not just one but several — in command of submarines when they were not qualified for the job. That may have been understandable at the start of the war, when we were shorthanded and had few qualified commanders. But after two years? There were many battle-tested officers who should have commanded submarines. That bothered me the most. Men's lives were at stake."

It is not the duty of a sailor to question the leadership, knowledge, or skill of his superior officers, though. It is the sailor's duty to obey orders and do what he was trained to do. That is one point Captain Rush always tries to make when he is speaking of the submarine service. It is not the boats; it is the men on those boats who do the job.

In 2002, Rush was in Hawaii for a special ceremony at a most historic spot. He was there to see his portrait added to the others that hang on the wall of the Clean Sweep Bar and Skippers' Lounge at Lockwood Hall, in the bachelor officers' quarters at Pearl Harbor. The room was a gathering place for submarine commanders to meet, relax, tell sea stories, and share details of their latest patrols and maneuvers. Rush's World War II–vintage photo was about to join those already on the wall. In so doing, he was about to share wall space with men like Admiral Charles Lockwood, Edward Beach, Dick O'Kane, and "Mush" Morton, men who were his heroes and role models as a young officer.

He told the assembled crowd, "When *Billfish* went through that long and difficult experience, I came to understand some things. The crew of the *Billfish* made that submarine."

But during his part of the ceremony, Rear Admiral John B. Padgett III, commander of the submarine force, U.S. Pacific fleet, best summed up what it meant to finally have the whole story of *Billfish* and her crew told.

"It is important that today's young officers and the wonderful young men they lead on those submarines understand the strength, the humility, and the courage of the men upon whose shoulders we all stand," Admiral Padgett said. "That legacy is profound. That legacy is what sustains us when times get tough today. The elements of courage that Captain Rush demonstrated as a young officer many years ago are those same elements we try to instill in our officers and the men they lead on our ships today."

Courage. Dedication. Pride.

Those were the hallmarks of the men who took the 286 boat to somewhere south of hell, and then brought her back again.

Just as Admiral Padgett noted, that is why it is so important that their story—the real story—can now be shared, not just for us but for those who go in harm's way on our behalf.

World War II lasted 1,347 days. During that time, 465 different submarine skippers took 263 different boats to battle on 1,736 war patrols. Approximately 16,000 men were riding along on those runs.

Over 4,000 merchant ships flying the Japanese flag were attacked, using almost 15,000 torpedoes. The American submarines sank nearly 1,200 of those merchantmen. They also sank over 200 naval vessels.

Of the 263 U.S. Navy submarines that went to war, 52 were lost. And with them, more than 3,600 men were dispatched on "eternal patrol."

A force that comprised less than 2 percent of the U.S. Navy during World War II was responsible for 55 percent of Japan's maritime losses. At the same time, with a casualty rate of over 20 percent, the submarine service had the highest mortality rate of any branch of the U.S. armed forces during the war.

When President Franklin Roosevelt saw the success and the heavy price paid by submariners, he said, "I can only echo the words of Winston Churchill. Never have so many owed so much to so few."

The submariners say it even more succinctly.

"Bravo Zulu."

"Job well-done."

AUTHOR'S NOTES

I n telling this remarkable story, I have necessarily relied on the memories of men who are in their eighties, men who are re-counting details of events that occurred more than sixty years ago, and who are attempting to recall experiences that happened under the most intense conditions anyone could possibly endure. Still, I am reasonably confident that these details are as accurate as I can make them and that the sources' recollections are true.

I say this because other research I have been able to obtain confirms their versions of events. I especially want to thank those who were so generous with their time and effort to assist in this project. That includes John Crouse, museum manager, St. Marys Submarine Museum in St. Marys, Georgia, who supplied excellent supporting documentation from their wonderful archives. Much of this material is now available online for anyone to access at the Historic Naval Ships Association's exceptional Web site at: http://www.hnsa.org/doc/subreports.htm.

My everlasting thanks as well go to Jon Jaques, submarine historian and archivist, a former submariner himself, and an officer in the United States Submarine Veterans organization. It was Jon who first told me the basics of this story. I'm a storyteller, and I was hooked immediately.

There is another connection here. Jon, my literary agent, Bob Robison, and I were in a car together en route to Arlington National Cemetery for the memorial service for Captain William R. Anderson. Bill was the man who took USS *Nautilus* to the North Pole in 1958 and with whom I cowrote an account of that remarkable voyage. He also made eleven World War II submarine patrols. Little did I know at the time that there would be a personal link between a diesel-powered submarine named *Billfish* and the amazing feat accomplished by the world's first nuclear-powered vessel. Only in my interviews with Captain Rush later did I learn of his early involvement in that historical event.

Jon, who is an accountant, has compiled a very precise history of World War II submarine captains, and I continue to rely on his work for fact-checking and other research.

Practically any work on World War II submarine warfare has to make use of the book *Silent Victory* by Clay Blair Jr. This one is no exception. Mr. Blair's exhaustive account of the various boats and patrols, captains and crew members, records and maneuverings, is an invaluable source. That applies not only to facts but also to personal accounts, anecdotes, and observations he culled from myriad sources in completing this amazing resource.

Some material in this book came from various newspaper articles, many of which appeared when the awards and citations were finally given to the key players in the story. That includes several articles by Navy personnel and in various base publications and some quotes from a story by Paul Reid of the *Palm Beach Post*. All of this material was later confirmed and expanded upon by Captain Charles Rush and others, in interviews I conducted with them or through other sources.

More details and quotes are based on an oral history given by Captain Rush to *Proceedings*, a publication of the Naval Institute, and an extensive oral history recorded by Chief Charley T. Odom for the University of Tennessee in Knoxville.

Thank you to both Charlie Rush and Charley Odom for leaving articles and oral histories so that the events of World War II can be preserved for future generations. The estimate is that we lose over a thousand World War II veterans a day. That represents a lot of history and many wonderful stories that we will never have documented.

I especially want to express my deepest appreciation to Charlie Rush for both his time and his infinite patience during his telephone interviews with me, and for his willingness to share this story with all of us.

Now, let me say that, with this book, I steam into shoaling waters on at least two courses.

First, and necessarily, I present as fact many details of events that are now almost sixty-five years old, but, as noted, I have tried to be as accurate as possible. In the course of telling the story, I also assign personality traits to and put words in the mouths of real men, most of whom have long since departed on "eternal patrol." Again, I have done my best to portray those men the way I believe they really were and not misrepresent them, their personalities, their words, or their actions in any way. Wherever possible, I wanted them to tell their story.

Second, I present in what might be considered an unflattering way several men who play important roles in this story. There was no way around it. As nearly as I can determine, this was very close to the way it happened. In every case, these were people who otherwise served their country well when they found themselves elsewhere besides on a submarine being pummeled by depth charges. I do not in any way want to diminish their contributions to the victory in World War II, nor what they did to preserve the peace afterward.

I am aware that these men have families, shipmates, and friends who will not necessarily appreciate the way they are depicted here. Again, I have tried to be as accurate and evenhanded in that portrayal as I could.

I also make the point in the narrative—and I am backed up by several of those who were there or who observed similar situations, as well as a consensus of historians—that many of these men were in the midst of something that few of us could have withstood. In addition, they were there through no fault of their own. Yes, they volunteered if they were in submarines. Still, they did not necessarily know there would be a war or that we would fight it the way this one was fought.

Usually, it was the higher-ups who made the bad decisions, placing the wrong men into positions of leadership. Then they were often too slow in correcting those questionable personnel moves.

It was those who faltered, though, who gave men like Charlie Rush, John Rendernick, Charley Odom, and the rest of the crew of *Billfish* the opportunity to show how brave men can be when they are thrust into such horrible, desperate situations.

This book is not about those who fell short. It is about those who excelled, who showed remarkable ingenuity and stirring bravery more than six hundred feet below the surface of a depth-charge-churned sea on Armistice Day 1943.

I dedicate this book to all of them and to the memories of those who are now gone.

Their courage and sacrifice should inspire us all. It certainly did me.

COMPLETE AND UNEDITED PATROL

REPORT FROM

USS *BILLFISH* FOR NOVEMBER 11, 1943

Proceeding through Macassar Strait, north of Cape William, on the surface at 14 knots.

0920   Sighted ship bearing 051°T, about 8 miles, which appeared to be a destroyer or smaller anti-submarine vessel, angle on the bow zero (Contact No. 1). Position 0-22S; 118-42E. Submerged immediately. The target maintained a steady course at high speed toward our diving point and was identified as a torpedo boat of about 225 feet in length, 3 stacks (the forward one split). Decided against torpedo attack due to small size and glassy sea which made periscope observations hazardous.

1407   Sighted smoke bearing 071°T (Contact No. 2). Commenced approach and target was made out to be another torpedo boat, probably Otori or Chidori class, making high speed.

1450   At a range of 3600, target appeared to have got by so abandoned approach. At this point he commenced pinging and turned toward us to present a 10 degree angle on the bow, at slow speed.

1500   Target showed zero angle, still pinging, so ordered 300 feet without increasing speed or using negative as it was still not believed that he had actual contact. Rigged ship for silent running and depth charge attack.

1505   While trying to get through layer at 200 feet heard screws pass overhead followed shortly by a barrage of 6 heavy charges which did considerable minor damage. Went to 400 feet and commenced evasion.

1640   After much leisurely listening and pinging during which the torpedo boat stayed right on top of us, received 6 more charges, apparently set deeper than the first, but we were then at 465 feet and they were less effective. Again heard screws through the hull before the charges. Shortly thereafter another A/S vessel joined in the hunt.

1900   Eight charges delivered by the two ships in a joint effort. After these reversed course through the disturbance and they lost contact for the first time.

12 November 1943.

0025   Surfaced in full moon and glassy sea and cleared the area.

APPENDIX II

Complete and Unedited Patrol

Report from

USS *Billfish* for November 28, 1943

0124   SJ Radar contact at 290°T, 14,000 yards. Five ships indicated. Commenced tracking and working for position ahead at 18 knots. Shortly thereafter picked up indications of BOWFIN's radar and at first believed she was also tracking convoy. However, after obtaining estimates of course, speed and composition of convoy asked BOWFIN by voice radio if she was on them. She replied that she had no targets so we gave her the position, course and speed estimate and our position, and learned that she was coming up from south about four miles inshore.

0249   Pinging commenced from direction of the convoy and radar picked up two more ships, smaller and closer. These believe to be escorts.

0300   (about) BOWFIN reported that she was in good position and asked permission to attack. Told her to go right ahead. She was on the inshore side with an excellent land mass and cloud background. We were unfortunately on the opposite side with a bright clear sky (the first in many days) in the background. We were also on the outside track as the convoy rounded Cape Varella.

0317-19   Observed and heard at least five torpedo explosions as BOW-FIN attacked. This was followed by gunfire, searchlights, and a few random depth charges. BOWFIN then reported the results of her attack as one sunk, two damaged and said she would wait for us. Also reported the two undamaged ships standing down toward us, 4-5000 yards apart. Commenced approach on the one to seaward. They had increased speed and were zig-zagging radically and independently.

0335   (about) BOWFIN reported that she only had two torpedoes left, suspected shell holes in her main induction, and was still in good position for an attack. Again told her to go right ahead.

0354   One of BOWFIN's last two torpedoes exploded at the end of the run in our vicinity giving us a jolt. BOWFIN then reported she was standing out to seaward.

0504   After considerable difficulty in attaining satisfactory firing position on the now very alert target, but with only a little darkness remaining, fired four torpedoes from the stern tubes with an estimated torpedo run of 3600 yards (Attack No. 1). Lost sight of target in land background just as firing was commenced and when next seen she had zigged about 30° away. Heard and felt one torpedo explosion which timed with correct torpedo run but target was then obscured by smoke from our engines as we went ahead for daylight position.

0620   By sunrise had not been able to gain position ahead of the target and knowing that there would be planes and more A/S vessels out from Camranh Bay, 40 miles away, soon after daylight, decided to submerge and try to close the coast to intercept one of the damaged ships coming down. Only the target we had chased was sighted, however, and he had changed course to far inshore. It is believed others did likewise.

0804   Heard pinging and sighted small patrol vessel searching about 3 miles inshore.

1310   Sighted single float seaplane at about 6 miles. Position 11-53N; 109-58E.

1845   Surfaced and set course to the eastward.

APPENDIX III

SELECTED NOTES FROM USS *BILLFISH*

REPORT OF SECOND WAR PATROL,

DATED DECEMBER 24, 1943

(J) ANTI-SUBMARINE MEASURES AND EVASION TACTICS.

The Otori or Chidori torpedo boat encountered on 11 November in Macassar Strait was remarkably effective both in original detection and in staying right on top of us for four hours.

Apparently he was aware of our presence in the vicinity, probably having been informed by aircraft, "spotters" on small sailing vessels, or by the first torpedo boat which we thought we had evaded without being detected. It is believed that he sighted our periscope at a range of approximately 3600 yards even though it was being used with extreme care because of the calm sea.

All attacks were very deliberate, unhurried, and well executed. He did not waste a charge. He sat for long periods almost directly over us, so that his auxiliaries could be plainly heard on the JP Sound Equipment, alternately listening and pinging, just kicking ahead occasionally to stay with us. All evasive maneuvers at silent speed were futile.

When entirely satisfied of our position he would start in for a run, but several times he apparently lost echo-ranging contact earlier than he expected because of our deep submergence (564-480 feet) and would stop and start the procedure all over again. This was especially aggravating as we had by this time become very heavy, requiring a 15° up angle to maintain depth, and were waiting for the next charges so that we could blow water from safety.

On each of the three dropping runs his screws were plainly heard through the hull 15-20 seconds before the charges.

The effectiveness of the attack seemed to be reduced rather than enhanced by the arrival of the second A/S vessel and contact was finally broken by doubling back through the disturbance caused by 8 charges dropped in a coordinated attack.

(K) MAJOR DEFECTS AND DAMAGE.

Major Defects:—None.

Damage—The only important damage from the depth charge attack on 11 November was the chipping and specking of the upper prism of number two periscope which made this periscope almost useless for the remainder of the patrol.

(P) HEALTH, FOOD AND HABITABILITY.

Health: The health of the crew was excellent. There were five admissions to the sick list with diagnosis and number of sick days as follows:

1 (officer) submersion	3 sick days.
1 (officer) intercranial injury	5 sick days.
3 Gonnoccus infection, urethea	0 sick days.
Total	8 sick days.

Food: The food was exceptionally well prepared and this compensated to a large degree for the absence of the fresh frozen and special foods which were available on the first patrol, having been obtained in the United States, but which were not available in Fremantle.

Habitability: Excellent.

(U) REMARKS.

(a) Conduct of Joint Patrol.

No opportunity was had to conclusively test the effectiveness of the joint patrol due to lack of contacts in the open sea where full advantage of the surface chase could be taken. On the occasion of the one contact when the two submarines were in contact BOWFIN completed a highly successful attack and expended the last of her torpedoes, but after one attack we were forced to submerge before obtaining satisfactory position for further attacks by the coming of daylight and the proximity of the shore and anti-submarine craft and aircraft.

The MN voice radio equipment was highly satisfactory for exchanging information on this contact. However plain language was used and it is doubtful whether this procedure could be used as freely, after the enemy discovers this equipment is being used, as it was on this occasion.

TEXT OF THE CITATIONS
ACCOMPANYING THE MEDALS AWARDED
TO CAPTAIN CHARLES W. RUSH AND
CHIEF JOHN RENDERNICK AND THE
CITATION TO
CHIEF CHARLEY ODOM

THE SECRETARY OF THE NAVY
WASHINGTON, D.C. 20305-1000
THE PRESIDENT OF THE UNITED STATES
TAKES PLEASURE IN PRESENTING THE
NAVY CROSS
TO
CAPTAIN CHARLES W. RUSH, JR.
UNITED STATES NAVY
FOR SERVICE SET FORTH IN THE FOLLOWING
CITATION:

For extraordinary heroism while serving as Chief Engineer and Diving Officer on Board USS BILLFISH (SS 286) during a combat war patrol in the enemy controlled waters of Makassar Strait on 11 November 1943. When an extremely severe depth charge attack incapacitated the Captain and all officers senior to Captain Rush (then Lieutenant Rush), with cool courage and outstanding professionalism he directed the damage control efforts directly responsible for saving the ship. The sustained accurate attacks caused major leaking through the stern tubes and various hull fittings and, it was later discovered, actually ruptured the pressure hull aft. Calling on his prior extensive combat experience, Captain Rush was able to maintain the submarine at 580 feet, almost 170 feet below her test depth, and prevent her sinking further to crush depth. During 12 straight exhaustive hours at his Diving Officer post, his calm demeanor, innovative damage control actions, and demonstrated courage in the face of perceived certain disaster served as the major inspiration to the crew to keep them functioning after most had given up all hope of survival. After finally being relieved by another officer, Captain Rush proceeded to the conning tower to assess the situation. He found the helm unmanned, the Captain and all senior officers still incapacitated, and no effective action being taken to counter the relentless depth charge attacks. Captain Rush, in a display of enlightened leadership, immediately assumed the conn, obtained a helmsman, and proceeded to direct evasive actions to elude the enemy above. Hearing the continuing explosions astern and reasoning that explosions close to the fuel ballast tanks had caused oil leaks that enabled the enemy ships to track the submarine's path, he then performed an innovative maneuver which resulted in the submarine retracing its own path in the opposite direction to pass under the old oil slicks. This so confused the enemy that they lost contact with the BILLFISH and Captain Rush was able to bring her to the surface after dark some four hours later, safely distant from the enemy now searching astern in a vain attempt to regain contact. He commenced recharging the depleted batteries with the single operable engine-generator and as more machinery was repaired he enhanced the propulsion capability and effected a successful escape from the scene. Captain Rush's inspiring and exceptional performance of duty under the worst imaginable conditions and in the face of seemingly certain death were directly responsible for saving BILLFISH and all hands from loss and for restoring the shattered confidence of the crew. By his courageous actions, superb leadership, and loyal dedication to duty, Captain Rush reflected great credit upon himself and upheld the highest traditions of the United States Naval Service.

For the President,
Gordon R. England
Secretary of the Navy

APPENDIX IV

POSTHUMOUS SILVER STAR MEDAL
CITATION FOR
CHIEF ELECTRICIAN'S MATE
JOHN D. RENDERNICK, USN

For conspicuous gallantry in action while serving on board USS *Billfish* (SS-286) during a combat war patrol in the enemy controlled waters of Makassar Strait on 11 November 1943. When a highly accurate enemy depth charge attack initially caused damage to the submarine's internal piping and hull fittings, subsequent semi-continuous severe attacks wrought major damage to all systems and vital equipment and put into question the submarine's survivability, Chief Petty Officer Rendernick immediately sprang into action from his battle station at the electrical control cubicle aft and commenced leading emergency repair efforts to reduce the heavy flooding through the stern tubes and to restore operability to such damaged equipment as possible. The severity of the situation was obvious to the crew, most of whom after eleven hours under constant attack gave up all hope of survival. Chief Petty Officer Rendernick displayed the highest degree of professionalism and leadership as he directed innovative damage control measures aft, including pumping grease into the worst leaking stern tube and utilizing six men and a hydraulic jack to reposition the port main motor, which had been knocked off its foundation by the shock of some extremely close depth charges, which had sheared its hold-down bolts. When the increasing pressure and heat reached the limit of the men's tolerance, Chief Petty Officer Rendernick had them wrap wet towels around their heads and take turns going into the more livable adjacent compartment for a rest. By his cool and courageous actions, exceptional initiative, and loyal dedication to duty, Chief Petty Officer Rendernick reflected great credit upon himself and upheld the highest traditions of the United States Naval Service.

THE DIRECTOR, SUBMARINE WARFARE DIVISION TAKES PLEASURE
IN COMMENDING
CHIEF ENGINEMAN (SUBMARINE SERVICE)
CHARLEY T. ODOM
UNITED STATES NAVY
FOR SERVICES AS SET FORTH IN THE FOLLOWING
CITATION:

For extraordinary service while serving as Chief Engineman on Board USS Billfish (SS 286) during a combat war patrol in the enemy controlled waters of Makassar Strait on 11 November 1943. When an extremely severe depth charge attack caused the stern tubes to spout water into the main motors, Chief Odom, standing in foot-deep water and wielding a large open-end wrench, tightened the nuts on the packing glands. As the submarine proceeded deep to evade the attack, Chief Odom was forced to loosen the nuts to stop them from smoking. For the next twelve hours, Chief Odom continued to tend the stern tubes while making frequent trips into the engine room to repair other leaks until the ship could safely surface. Upon surfacing, three of the four main engines were flooded and would not start. Chief Odom, exhibiting detailed knowledge of the complicated procedure, one-by-one rapidly restarted the engines so that propulsion and battery charging could be accomplished before daybreak. Chief Odom's courageous actions and loyal dedication to duty reflected great credit upon himself and upheld the highest traditions of the United States Naval Service.

(Signed)
P. F. SULLIVAN
Rear Admiral, U.S. Navy

APPENDIX V

GLOSSARY OF
WORLD WAR II SUBMARINE TERMS

1-MC—The shipwide intercom system aboard submarines.

Aft—The rearmost section of a ship.

After Battery Compartment—Main section of the submarine behind the control room. This area housed battery cells and the enlisted men's living and dining spaces.

Annunciator—An electromechanical signaling device used to send orders to the engine room and maneuvering room.

Ash Cans—Slang term for depth charges.

Astern—A position or location behind the ship.

ASW, A/S—Antisubmarine warfare.

Ballast—Tanks are filled with seawater, which acts as weight, causing the submarine to lose buoyancy and sink. To surface, compressed air is pumped into the tanks, forcing the seawater out and restoring positive buoyancy.

Battle Stations—Preassigned places throughout the ship where crew members work during engagements with the enemy.

Beam—Measured dimension of a ship at its widest part.

Bearing—The direction to a target in relation to the ship. For example, a target that was directly ahead would have a bearing of zero degrees.

Bilge—Lower part of the submarine where wastewater and seepage collect.

Blowing—Blowing a tank means expelling its contents by pumping compressed air into the tank to force out the water.

Bow—The nose or front of a ship.

Brag Rags—Miniature Japanese flags displayed on the conning tower or flown from the periscope shears of World War II U.S. submarines indicating the number of enemy vessels she had sunk.

Bridge—On a submarine, the small observation area on top of the sail, just above the conning tower.

Brow—A gangplank, ladder, or walkway leading from the submarine to the pier.

Bubble, Down—A device used to measure the degree of downward incline when diving a submarine.

Bubble, "Ease the bubble." "Zero bubble." "Five degrees down bubble."—Orders to the stern planesman giving the angle of the dive or surfacing that is desired.

Bubble, Up—Device used to measure the degree of upward incline when surfacing a submarine.

Chief of the Boat, COB—A petty officer in charge of enlisted personnel. This sailor was generally one of the most experienced of the enlisted men on board.

Christmas Tree—The indicator light panel that shows the status of the various hull openings. The lights are red and green.

Cigarette Deck—The open, railed platform aft of a U.S. fleet submarine's bridge.

Class—Ship types are assigned to various classes based on type of construction and mission assignment. In the U.S. Navy, the name of the first vessel constructed within each class is assigned to the class. USS *Billfish*, for example, was a *Balao*-class submarine because USS *Balao* was the first boat in her class.

Compensation—The process of transferring ballast, in the form of water, between the variable tanks and between the variable tanks and sea, all to keep the boat level or at the proper attitude for diving or surfacing.

Conn, Conning Tower—The control room from which navigation and attacks were directed. It was most heavily used while operating at periscope depth.

Control Room—The compartment just below the conning tower that contained all diving controls, the ship's gyrocompass and its auxiliary, the air search radar, an auxiliary steering stand, the interior communications switchboard, and the radio room.

CPO—Chief petty officer.

Damage Control—Measures necessary to keep a ship afloat and in operational condition.

Depth Charge—Explosive charge used against submarines.

Destroyer—A naval vessel, usually equipped for either ASW or antiair operations. Sometimes referred to as a "tin can."

Displacement—The weight of a boat or ship, as measured by the amount of water displaced when placing the vessel in water.

Diving Officer—The officer on a submarine responsible for overseeing the submerging and surfacing of the boat as well as maintaining the desired depth.

Diving Trim—The condition of a submarine when flooding main ballast, safety, and bow buoyancy tanks so that the submarine will submerge with neutral buoyancy and zero fore and aft trim.

Dogs—The hardware that secures a watertight door or hatch.

"Dolphins"—Pins worn by submariners indicating they have "qualified in submarines."

Emergency Blow—Command to release ballast from a submarine by rapidly pumping compressed air into ballast tanks, no matter how much noise may be generated in the process. This forces seawater out of the ballast tanks and enables an endangered submarine to reach the surface.

Engine Induction Valve, Main Induction—Large valve that provides airflow to the diesel engines.

Escort—A ship or aircraft used to protect merchant ships, warships, or convoys.

Fathom—Six feet or 1.829 meters of water depth.

Final Trim—When the fore and aft and overall weights are adjusted so that the boat maintains the desired depth on an even keel at slow speed and with minimum use of the diving planes.

Fire Control—The mechanics of directing torpedoes or gunfire. Often refers to all crew members who participated in firing torpedoes.

Flooding—Filling a tank.

Flood Valves—Covers at the bottom of certain ballast tanks that are opened to admit or push out seawater.

Galley—A ship's kitchen.

Gradient—A layer where the temperature of the seawater, and to a lesser degree its density, changes abruptly, thus sending sound waves of echo-ranging in a different direction, effectively hiding a submarine below the layer.

Green Board—The report that indicates all hull openings are shut, as shown on the hull opening indicator panel, or "Christmas tree."

Gyrocompass—A compass that receives its directional information from a rapidly spinning gyroscope driven by electric motors. Its directive action is determined by the mechanical laws governing the dynamics of rotating bodies.

Head—Naval term for a toilet.

Helm—The mechanism for steering a submarine, the wheel.

Helmsman—Crew member responsible for maintaining the direction of travel of the submarine.

Knot—A measurement of speed equal to one nautical mile per hour.

Maneuver—A change of speed, course, or formation to adjust position or take a new position.

Mess—To eat; a group of men eating together.

Mess Deck—Location of the crew's eating area, in the aft battery.

Momsen Lung—A breathing apparatus to permit an individual to breathe normally while escaping from a sunken submarine. It also serves as a gas mask in the submarine and as a life preserver on the surface. Named for submariner Charles "Swede" Momsen, who invented the device.

Officer of the Deck, OOD—An officer on duty aboard a submarine who is acting as the commanding officer's representative, usually in the conn.

"Old Man"—A seaman's term for the captain of the ship.

On Watch—A sailor's assigned period for being on duty, at work.

Outer Doors—Doors in the hull of a submarine covering the exit of the torpedo tubes. These had to be open to the sea in order to fire torpedoes.

PCO—Prospective commanding officer of a submarine.

Periscope—An optical instrument that allowed submarines, while remaining submerged, to view activity on or above the surface. *Billfish* had two periscopes.

Periscope Depth—The depth at which a submerged submarine can extend its periscope above the surface of the sea.

Picket—A ship stationed for the purpose of picking up by radar the approach of the enemy.

Pinging—Distinctive sound generated by an active sonar system.

Planes, Bow—Horizontal rudders, or diving planes, extending from each side of the outside of the submarine near the bow.

Planes, Stern—Horizontal rudders, or diving planes, extending from each side of the the outside of the submarine near the stern.

Port—The left side of a ship relative to someone who is facing forward, toward the bow.

Pressure Hull—The submarine's inner hull and conning tower, built of heavy steel to withstand the sea pressure.

Pumping—Employing a pump to transfer liquid from the tank to sea, from the sea into a tank, or from one tank to another.

Quick Dive—Quickly submerging a submarine while running on its main engines.

Radar, SD—Nondirectional radar that could basically tell that an aircraft was approaching but not with any accuracy as to its direction.

Radar, SJ—Directional radar, which could be used to sweep the surrounding sea for targets. SJ radar was designed for search, ranging, and navigation. In addition to conducting surface searches, the radar masts could also be extended above the water before surfacing to check the area for enemy warships and aircraft.

Rag Hat—Slang term for an enlisted submariner.

"Rig for . . ."—Command for the ship to be placed into some specified condition, as in "Rig for dive," or "Rig for silent running."

Rig for Dive—Preparing the hull openings and machinery so the submarine can be quickly and safely submerged and controlled by flooding the main ballast tanks, using the diving planes, and operating on the main electric motors.

Rudder—A movable paddle at the stern of a submarine, used to determine the lateral direction of travel.

Running Dive—Submerging a submarine while running on battery power.

Sail—The portion of a submarine above the main deck, including the conning tower.

Screw—The device that, when turned by the ship's engines, propels a submarine through the water. Sometimes called the "propeller."

Shears—The radio and radar antennas, periscope housings, searchlight, flagpoles, and lookout stands that tower high above the decks and water.

Silent Running—A condition under which all nonessential machinery and equipment is shut down in order to minimize the noise generated by a submarine. The object is to minimize the possibility of detection by a surface vessel or another submarine.

Snorkel—A device extended above the surface from a submerged submarine to allow air to be pumped into the submerged submarine. This made it possible to run the submarine's diesel engines so the batteries could be recharged.

Sonar—Technology that relies on underwater sound propagation for navigation, communication, or detection of other vessels. SOund NAvigation and Ranging.

Starboard—The right side of a ship relative to a person who is facing forward, toward the bow.

Stationary Dive—Submerging a submarine while the boat is not moving forward or backward but is stationary in the water.

Stern—The rear section or tail of a submarine.

Submarine Tender—An auxiliary vessel that supplies and repairs submarines.

Submerged Condition—A condition in which all of the vessel is completely submerged with the variable ballast set so that the submarine has neutral buoyancy and zero fore and aft trim.

Surface Condition—When the ship has sufficient positive buoyancy after surfacing to be able to safely run on the main engines.

Tank, Auxiliary—Variable ballast tanks located at the submerged center of buoyancy, used to adjust the overall trim of the boat.

Tank, Battery Freshwater—Storage tanks for the distilled water used in the main storage batteries.

Tank, Bow Buoyancy—A tank with its main volume above the normal surface waterline, it is in the bow of the submarine. It provides reserve surface buoyancy, emergency positive buoyancy in the submerged condition, and helps during surfacing.

Tank, Clean Fuel Oil—Storage tanks located within the pressure hull, they are where the engines draw their clean fuel.

Tank, Expansion—Receive overflow from the fuel tanks and input from bilges that is pumped in to prevent leaving an oil slick or polluting a harbor.

Tank, Freshwater—Contain water to be used for drinking, cooking, and sanitary facilities.

Tank, Fuel Ballast—Used as auxiliary fuel oil tanks for increased operating range. When empty, they can be used as main ballast tanks.

Tank, Fuel Oil—Contain engine fuel oil and, since they are located outside the pressure hull, they cannot take the pressure of the sea during a dive. They must always be filled with fuel oil or water. As fuel is used from these tanks, it is replaced with seawater. Fuel oil floats on water and is withdrawn from the top of the tank.

Tank, Main Ballast—Tanks that furnish buoyancy when the vessel is on the surface.

Tank, Negative—A variable ballast tank that gives negative buoyancy and initial down-angle. It is used to reduce the time required in submerging and to prevent broaching when decreasing depth.

Tank, Safety—A heavily reinforced main ballast tank used to quickly regain positive buoyancy.

Tank, Sanitary—Stores sanitary drainage until it can be discharged overboard.

Tank, Trim—Variable ballast tanks at the bow and stern that are used to keep the boat at the desired attitude.

Tank, Variable Ballast—Ballast tanks whose contents can vary for weight compensation and are built to withstand full sea pressure.

Tank, WRT (water 'round torpedoes)—Variable ballast tanks in the forward and after torpedo rooms for flooding or draining the torpedo tubes. When a torpedo is fired, water equal to the weight of the torpedo is pumped into the WRT tank to compensate for the loss of weight.

Target Bearing Transmitter (TBT)—A permanently mounted binocular instrument that can be used to sight objects and determine their bearing relative to the heading of the submarine.

Topside—Exposed or semiexposed, nonwatertight areas of the ship, usually referring to the main deck.

Torpedo Data Computer (TDC)—Electromechanical analog computer used for torpedo fire control on American submarines during World War II. The submarine's course and speed were read automatically from the boat's compass and other equipment, but information for the target's bearing and speed had to be entered manually. The firing solution was then sent through an electromechanical link to the torpedoes themselves, and could be updated by observations right up until the torpedo was fired.

Torpedo Room—The compartments in a submarine designed for the storage, maintenance, and launching of torpedoes. Most submarines had two torpedo rooms, one at the rear and one at the front of the boat.

Torpedo Run—The distance in yards that a torpedo travels from the tube to the target.

True Bearing—Gyrocompass bearing, or bearings in degrees measured clockwise from earth's true north. Usually abbreviated "T" in deck logs and patrol reports.

Venting—Allowing the flow of air into or out of a tank.

Vents, Emergency—Stop valves near the tank tops used in case of damage to the main vents to prevent accidental flooding.

Vents, Main—Valves for venting the main ballast tanks when flooding.

Wardroom—The dining area and social center for officers on a submarine. Also used generically to refer to all officers collectively aboard a submarine.

Watch Section—The officers and men on duty in a specified area constitute the watch section for that area.

Wolf Pack—Several submarines acting as a unit.

INDEX

Index